T0323997

Cambridge Elements ≡

Elements in Applied Linguistics
edited by
Li Wei
University College London
Zhu Hua
University College London

INVESTIGATING PLAGIARISM IN SECOND LANGUAGE WRITING

Jun Lei
Ningbo University

Guangwei Hu
The Hong Kong Polytechnic University

CAMBRIDGE
UNIVERSITY PRESS

Shaftesbury Road, Cambridge CB2 8EA, United Kingdom

One Liberty Plaza, 20th Floor, New York, NY 10006, USA

477 Williamstown Road, Port Melbourne, VIC 3207, Australia

314–321, 3rd Floor, Plot 3, Splendor Forum, Jasola District Centre,
New Delhi – 110025, India

103 Penang Road, #05–06/07, Visioncrest Commercial, Singapore 238467

Cambridge University Press is part of Cambridge University Press & Assessment,
a department of the University of Cambridge.

We share the University's mission to contribute to society through the pursuit of
education, learning and research at the highest international levels of excellence.

www.cambridge.org
Information on this title: www.cambridge.org/9781009571692

DOI: 10.1017/9781009350822

First published 2024

A catalogue record for this publication is available from the British Library

ISBN 978-1-009-57169-2 Hardback
ISBN 978-1-009-35085-3 Paperback
ISSN 2633-5069 (online)
ISSN 2633-5050 (print)

Cambridge University Press & Assessment has no responsibility for the persistence
or accuracy of URLs for external or third-party internet websites referred to in this
publication and does not guarantee that any content on such websites is, or will
remain, accurate or appropriate.

Investigating Plagiarism in Second Language Writing

Elements in Applied Linguistics

DOI: 10.1017/9781009350822
First published online: December 2024

Jun Lei
Ningbo University

Guangwei Hu
The Hong Kong Polytechnic University

Author for correspondence: Jun Lei, leijun@nbu.edu.cn

Abstract: This Element aims to provide a comprehensive and in-depth exploration of the issue of plagiarism in second language writing. It first outlines the importance of plagiarism as a real-world issue cutting across educational and cultural contexts and touches upon several prominent controversies over the issue. Then the Element defines and conceptualises plagiarism by critically examining the diverse extant definitions and discussing various discourses on plagiarism. Following that, it explores L2 students' perceptions of and stances on plagiarism, and identifies factors that contribute to L2 students' plagiarism. Informed by the current theoretical and empirical research, the Element critically evaluates three major approaches to dealing with plagiarism and, based on the critical evaluation, proposes pedagogical activities and strategies for fostering L2 students' intertextual competence. Finally, the Element calls for a reconceptualisation of plagiarism that embraces a multidimensional approach to dealing with plagiarism in second language writing, and outlines directions for further research.

Keywords: plagiarism, second language writing, patchwriting, inadvertent plagiarism, source use

ISBNs: 9781009571692 (HB), 9781009350853 (PB), 9781009350822 (OC)
ISSNs: 2633-5069 (online), 2633-5050 (print)

Contents

1 Introduction

Plagiarism is a perennial source of concern for educational institutions, educators, and students. The media and academia have long sounded an alarm about the widespread of plagiarism, which is said to have escalated into a plagiarism epidemic (Howard et al., 2010) or caused a plagiarism-related moral panic (Clegg & Flint, 2006). Plagiarism has also evoked strong emotions among various stakeholders. Instructors may feel upset, hurt, or insulted when they find plagiarism in their students' assignments (Kolich, 1983), and some may feel torn as to whether to report it to the authorities (Howard, 1999; Pecorari, 2013; Valentine, 2006). Specifically, they may 'feel betrayed (by the student's deception), angered (by the student's laziness), and disappointed (by the student's lack of learning)' (Valentine, 2006, p. 96). Students may also experience emotional turbulence if they are caught and accused of plagiarising (Abasi & Akbari, 2008; East, 2006; Leask, 2006). Institutions, too, often express indignance at students' intentional plagiarism and take a punitive stance towards it (Sun & Hu, 2024).

It has been suggested that advances in information technology have made it increasingly easier to cut and paste others' work and pass it off as one's own, a development that has often been cited as a cause of increasingly rampant plagiarism (Husain et al., 2017; Selwyn, 2008; Walker, 2010). A case in point is the leaps and bounds that generative AI has made in the past few years and the potential use of large language models' generated outputs to facilitate plagiarism (Dehouche, 2021; Eke, 2023). However, with the emergence of plagiarism detection or text-matching tools, technological development has also played a role in detecting and curtailing the spread of plagiarism (Flowerdew & Li, 2007b; Park, 2003; Robillard & Howard, 2008). As highlighted in ongoing discussion, the recent advances of generative AI (e.g., ChatGPT) have further complicated the issue of plagiarism and given rise to a number of ethical concerns, including ownership of the content generated by a large language model, citation practices, issues of copyright, among others (Cotton et al., 2024; Eke, 2023; Lund et al., 2023). In response to these concerns, various detectors of AI-generated texts have been or are being developed, though their accuracy and reliability still leave much to be desired currently (Weber-Wulff et al., 2023). As such detectors need to be trained on the outputs of large language models that they aim to detect, they seem to be destined to play the role of catching up with the increasing sophistication and complexity of the generating models, leading to a cat and mouse game (Fröhling & Zubiaga, 2021).

Aside from the technology-related challenges, there is another long-standing controversy over the role of culture in shaping second language (L2) students' perceptions and practices of plagiarism (Deckert, 1993; Matalene, 1985; Pennycook, 1994). One side of this controversy opines that plagiarism is understood and interpreted differently in different cultures, and thus culturally conditioned (Sowden, 2005). From this cultural-conditioning view, Asian students in general and Chinese students in particular are inclined to plagiarise because of their cultural values, literacy traditions, and textual practices (Hayes & Introna, 2005a; Pennycook, 1996; Scollon, 1995). Taken to the extreme, this view essentialises the role of culture, asserting that Chinese culture in particular and Asian cultures in general condone and accept plagiarism (Flowerdew & Li, 2007b; Lei & Hu, 2015).

However, scholars (e.g., Liu, 2005; Phan, 2006) have questioned the validity of the cultural-conditioning view, arguing that apart from cultural factors, there are many other contributors to L2 students' plagiarism, including inadequate language proficiency, limited task-specific writing skills, unfamiliarity with the L2 writing conventions, and the temptation to cheat. As Liu (2005) observes, 'inadequate language proficiency and writing skills may be the main reason for Asian ESOL [English for Speakers of Other Languages] students' plagiarism problem' (p. 239). Phan (2006) challenges the tendency to see reputedly cultural practices of 'obedience to authority and lack of critical thinking' as contributors to Asian students' propensity to plagiarise (p. 77). She points out that the tendency runs the risk of stereotyping Asian cultures and students and constitutes a misinterpretation of the role of culture in plagiarism. Based on her comprehensive analysis of textual materials including texts from classical Chinese, Li (2024) demonstrates that plagiarism was condemned in China since antiquity. Additionally, Liu (2005) problematises the cultural-conditioning view for its inability to offer pedagogical implications because it often ends by 'treating the problem as a language and writing development issue rather than a cultural one' (pp. 239–240).

Still another controversy concerns the question of what an effective solution to the problem of student plagiarism is. The earliest proposals to curtail plagiarism advocated a 'Gotcha' approach to catch and punish offenders without ruth (Kolich, 1983; Price, 2002). Subsequently, it was proposed that the detection and punishment approach should be replaced with one that would pivot on ethics education and appeal to students' sense of academic integrity and honour to keep clear of plagiaristic behaviours (McCabe, 2001). More recently, there have been calls for pedagogical interventions oriented to equipping students with the knowledge, skills, and strategies needed to engage in legitimate intertextuality (Hu, 2015b; Pecorari & Petrić, 2014). Up-to-date, however, empirical research is lacking that systematically compares the effectiveness of these approaches. As will be further discussed later, given the multiple and complex causes of plagiarism, it makes sense to expect the various approaches to differ in their effectiveness in addressing plagiarism stemming from different factors (Hu & Lei, 2015).

The complexity of plagiarism has prompted researchers to investigate it from multiple perspectives, including cultural, moral, and developmental perspectives (Flowerdew & Li, 2007b; Pecorari & Petrić, 2014). The cultural perspective asserts that plagiarism is a culturally conditioned practice, with some cultures (e.g., Confucian heritage cultures) accepting of it (Sowden, 2005). However, research (e.g., Chandrasegaran, 2000; Lei & Hu, 2015; Wheeler, 2009) has yielded evidence against this cultural essentialist view of plagiarism. This research shows that different cultures may conceptualise plagiarism differently, but having different conceptualisations of plagiarism is not equal to condoning or accepting of plagiarism (Hu & Lei, 2012; Scollon, 1995; Wheeler, 2009). The moral perspective holds that plagiarism is a moral transgression and should thus be punished categorically (Briggs, 2003; Valentine, 2006). Different from the cultural and moral perspectives, the developmental perspective views plagiarism as a developmental issue in need of pedagogical intervention (Howard, 1999; Pecorari, 2023). This perspective posits that students learn by imitating others' work and are predisposed to patchwrite (i.e., copy others' work and replace some of its words with one's own), which is a natural process of learning and a transitional stage for novice writers (Campbell, 1990; Gu & Brooks, 2008; Howard, 1993; Pecorari, 2003).

An examination of decades of research indicates that it is vital to adopt a multidimensional approach to understanding and dealing with student plagiarism. In this regard, some researchers (e.g., Chandrasoma et al., 2004; Pecorari, 2001; Sutherland-Smith, 2005; Valentine, 2006) have highlighted the importance of addressing the moral connotations of plagiarism and differentiating advertent and inadvertent intertextual transgression. To that end, a wide array of terms has been proposed, including patchwriting (Howard, 1993; Pecorari, 2003), language reuse (Flowerdew & Li, 2007a), language/textual borrowing (Barks & Watts, 2001; Shi, 2004), transgressive and non-transgressive intertextuality (Borg, 2009; Chandrasoma et al., 2004), among others. For example, in view of the derogatory connotations of plagiarism, Chandrasoma et al. (2004) suggest 'do[ing] away with the notion of plagiarism in favour of an understanding of transgressive or nontransgressive intertextuality' (p. 171). Thus, while it is reasonable to punish students who plagiarise intentionally or engage in transgressive intertextual practices knowingly, a pedagogical or remedial approach should be taken to deal with unintentional plagiarism (Du, 2022; Pecorari, 2013; Price, 2002; Tomaš, 2010). In relation to this, there is also a call for reforming institutional policies to recognise the complexity of plagiarism and to avoid a purely detecting-and-punishing approach to plagiarism (Hu & Sun, 2017; Pecorari, 2013). As a result, some researchers (e.g., Hayes & Introna, 2005b; Li & Casanave, 2012; McCulloch et al., 2022) have proposed to use plagiarism detection software as a pedagogical tool, rather than a 'breathalyser', to help students learn about legitimate source-use practices. Other researchers (e.g., Howard et al., 2010; Hu, 2015b; Pecorari, 2013) have stressed the need to provide students with academic writing instruction and assistance, which can guide students to use sources appropriately and effectively.

To summarise, despite extensive research attention to student plagiarism over the past three decades or so, we still lack a comprehensive knowledge about various aspects of this complex phenomenon, for example, 'the prevalence and causes of plagiarism' or 'effective pedagogical methods' for addressing it (Pecorari, 2023, p. 362). In light of the complex and multidimensional nature of plagiarism, it is crucial to reconceptualise it by taking into account various perspectives on it. Approaches to addressing it should also be recalibrated to align with its reconceptualisation. To these ends, this Element aims to (1) provide an up-to-date discussion on plagiarism that deals with both conceptual and pedagogical issues, and (2) offer a point of departure for various stakeholders to grasp the complexities of plagiarism and tackle the issue from the perspectives of both policy and pedagogy. The unique feature of the Elements series enables us to provide a comprehensive yet accessible overview of the major issues surrounding plagiarism in second language writing that differs from those provided by existing review articles and books on plagiarism.

This section has underlined the importance of plagiarism as a real-world issue, sketched out several controversies over it, and concluded with a call for reconceptualising it and recalibrating approaches to tackling it. Section 2 scrutinises extant definitions and conceptualisations of plagiarism in the literature, and highlights the complex and multifaceted nature of plagiarism in second language writing. In Section 3, we explore students' perceptions of and stances on plagiarism, point out a problematic tendency in extant research to conflate L2 students' knowledge of and stance on plagiarism, and underscore the need to differentiate the two. To extend the discussion, four sets of factors that contribute to L2 students' plagiarism are examined in Section 4. Following that, Section 5 surveys three major approaches to dealing with plagiarism and proposes pedagogical activities and strategies for helping L2 students steer clear of plagiarism and improve their intertextual competence. Finally, Section 6 concludes this Element with a reconceptualisation of plagiarism and an outline of directions for further research.

2 Defining and Conceptualising Plagiarism

2.1 Definitions of Plagiarism

The literature has suggested that it is extremely challenging, if not impossible, to define plagiarism (Buranen & Roy, 1999; Howard, 1999; Price, 2002). There is no consensus on the definition of plagiarism in academia, to say the least (Briggs, 2003; Gu & Brooks, 2008; Pennycook, 1996). Pecorari (2001) notes that plagiarism is 'anything but a cut-and-dried concept' (p. 241). Furthermore, as Scollon (1995) observes, public discourse on plagiarism has focused on two main issues, namely the degree of similarity between a text and its source(s) and the intentionality of the author. However, the literature has shown that there is no clear boundary between legitimate and illegitimate textual borrowing (Howard, 1995, 1999; Pecorari, 2003, 2006). Shi (2010), for example, points out that what constitutes appropriate and inappropriate textual borrowing 'is negotiated, localized, and contingent' (p. 22). There is also controversy over the necessity of using intention as a criterion for defining and ascertaining plagiarism because despite its importance, it is intrinsically difficult to diagnose or establish it without the author's own revelation (Pecorari, 2001; Sutherland-Smith, 2005). As noted by Howard (1999), 'plagiarism policies may even specifically exclude the writer, stipulating that plagiarism is plagiarism even if the writer is ignorant of its prohibitions' (p. 108). Due to its indeterminate and elusive nature, the author's intention is often inferred from the features of the text and is thus frequently used as a convenient label for texts rather than authors (Howard, 1999; Roy, 1999). Such inferences, however, contribute to much uncertainty about the concept of plagiarism (Yeo, 2007).

There are a multitude of challenges in defining plagiarism. One has to do with the origin of the concept. The etymology of the word *plagiarism* can be traced back to the ancient Latin word *plagiarius*, which literally means 'kidnapper' and is used to refer to the stealing of slaves and words (Howard, 1995). As such, the Western notion of plagiarism has cultural and ideological baggage and reflects particular cultural and ideological positionings (Currie, 1998; Pennycook, 1996; Scollon, 1995). It is closely tied to the notions of authorship, authenticity, intellectual property, and copyright, which may not be shared or understood in the same way by other cultures (Pennycook, 1996; Scollon, 1995). The concept of plagiarism is thus premised on proprietorship, originality, and autonomy. 'If there is no originality, there is no basis for literary property. If there is no originality and no literary property, there is no basis for the notion of plagiarism', as aptly put by Howard (1995, p. 791). Furthermore, the concept of plagiarism is also underpinned by the assumption of autonomous, creative, and rational individuals 'as originators of their own discourses' (Scollon,

1995, p. 1). However, scholars (e.g., Lundsford, 1999; Pennycook, 1996; Scollon, 1995) have called into question the notion of individual ownership of texts. Specifically, the notion is at odds with the dialogic or derivative nature of language, which dictates that our language is always 'filled with others' words' and hetero-glossic as a result of our efforts to assimilate others' discourse and make it our own (Bakhtin, 1986, p. 89; see also Howard, 1999; Pennycook, 1996; Scollon, 1995).

Another challenge in defining plagiarism relates to, as noted by Pecorari (2001) and Sutherland-Smith (2005), the difficulty in pinning down the intention of the perpetrator. Despite the widely held belief that there is no such thing as unintentional plagiarism, research has suggested that some transgressive intertextual practices are not engaged in intentionally to cheat (Howard, 1999; Pecorari, 2008; Shi, 2010). Studies examining students' writing and source texts closely have pointed to the existence of unintentional plagiarism (Flowerdew & Li, 2007a; Pecorari, 2003, 2006). Pecorari (2003), for example, compared the excerpts of seventeen graduate students' theses with the original sources and found that sixteen theses had one or more passages that copied fifty or more of the words from the sources without attribution. However, the students did not seem to have any intention to deceive as evidenced in both the texts and the interviews with them. Similarly, interview-based studies of students' views on plagiarism have also identified indications of unintentional plagiarism (Angélil-Carter, 2000; Chandrasoma et al., 2004; Currie, 1998; Starfield, 2002). For this reason, as pointed out in the earlier section, various alternative terms have been proposed to replace plagiarism. For instance, Howard (1999) has put forward the notion of patchwriting, which is defined as 'copying from a source text and then deleting some words, altering grammatical structures, or plugging in one synonym for another' (p. xvii). As Howard further notes, patchwriting with acknowledgement would still be considered plagiarism according to traditional definitions of plagiarism.

It is thus imperative to draw a fine line between plagiarism and cheating on exams or purchasing term papers as well as between intentional and unintentional plagiarism. In particular, to differentiate intentional and unintentional plagiarism, Pecorari (2008) proposes a two-level typology of textual plagiarism, which involves 'the use of words and/or ideas from another source, without appropriate attribution' (p. 4). Her typology divides textual plagiarism into two subtypes: prototypical plagiarism (characterised by an intention to deceive) and patchwriting (where no such intention is present). Focusing predominantly on textual features (i.e., the similarity or lack of similarity between texts), this two-level classification of textual plagiarism 'allows for discussions of source-use and textual analysis without reference to the writer's intention to deceive or the need to establish it, while at the same time opening up the possibility of taking intent into consideration if it can be established' (Pecorari & Petrić, 2014, p. 276).

A third and related challenge in defining plagiarism concerns the multifarious forms that it can take. Research (e.g., Chandrasegaran, 2000; Hu & Lei, 2012; Wheeler, 2009) has shown that plagiarism can come in various forms, ranging from blatant word-for-word copying without acknowledgement to inadequate paraphrasing with full acknowledgement. Abasi and Akbari (2008), for example, distinguish localised and global patchwriting, with the former defined as 'close appropriation at the micro level of lexis and syntax' (p. 270) and the latter as 'ineffective appropriation at the level of ideas' (p. 271). It is thus vital to adopt a fine-grained approach to defining plagiarism. Such an approach needs to first acknowledge that not all cases of textual borrowing are intended to deceive and then stipulate that a nuanced differentiation of different types of plagiarism be adopted.

Despite the difficulties in defining it and the lack of an agreed-upon understanding of it, plagiarism can be defined 'in a robust and defensible way' (Pecorari, 2023, p. 363). Drawing on a survey of policies on plagiarism gathered from universities in the US, the UK, and Australia, Pecorari (2001) identifies six common elements in the definitions of plagiarism found in these policies, including '(1) material that has been (2) taken from (3) some source by (4) someone, (5) without acknowledgment and (6) with/without intention to deceive' (p. 235). In light of these and other empirically verified elements, Pecorari (2013) proposes four criteria for defining plagiarism, namely similarity between two texts, the later text being based on the earlier one, the intertextual relationship being inappropriate, and intention to deceive. Complementary to Pecorari's approach to defining plagiarism by focusing on common elements and criteria for such definitions is an alternative line of research that tries to uncover the larger discourses – 'ways of thinking, believing, valuing, and using various symbols, tools, and objects' (Gee, 2011, p. 201) – within which particular definitions are embedded to capture broader conceptions of plagiarism. Three distinct discourses on plagiarism are discernible and are labelled, respectively, as the moral, regulatory, and developmental discourses (Adam et al., 2017; Hu & Sun, 2017; Kaposi & Dell, 2012; Pan & Lei, 2024). It is to these discourses that we turn next.

2.2 The Moral Discourse

There is a received view among both academia and the public that plagiarism is a moral transgression and an intentional act that warrants sanctions (Cumming et al., 2016; Flowerdew & Li, 2007b; Pecorari & Petrić, 2014). As noted in Section 1, part of the literature portrays plagiarism as a 'moral panic' (Clegg & Flint, 2006) or an 'epidemic' (Howard et al., 2010). In a systematic review of fifty-five research articles on plagiarism in higher education from 1982 to 2022, McKenna (2022, p. 1) found that most of the articles adopted 'a police-catch-punish approach' to plagiarism and were laden with 'a moral charge'. Thus, this discourse tends to use a highly charged language to caricature the prevalence of plagiarism and ascribe the perceived increase in the incidence of plagiarism among students to their deteriorating moral standards (Kaposi & Dell, 2012; Pecorari & Petrić, 2014). Specifically, the moral discourse typically makes an exorbitant use of moral and/or legal language to characterise plagiarism as an intentional, dishonest, immoral, and reprehensible act (Adam et al., 2017; Merkel, 2021). The moral parlance relates plagiarism to immorality, misconduct, dishonesty and deceit, whereas the legal vocabulary associates it with copyright, breach, defraud, and theft (Ashworth et al., 1997; McCabe, 2005a; Park, 2003; Yeo, 2007). As Kaposi and Dell (2012) point out, 'the bedrock of this discourse is the unquestionable intention of the agent' (p. 816). Thus, the moral discourse views all forms of plagiarism categorically as immoral and dishonest (Hu & Sun, 2017).

On the one hand, plagiarism is portrayed as 'a moral maze, because it raises important ethical and moral questions about good/bad or right/wrong behaviour and about acceptable/unacceptable practices' (Park, 2003, p. 475). The logic underlying the moral discourse on plagiarism is that 'one plagiarizes to get out of doing work and, therefore, should be punished' (Valentine, 2006, p. 96). Thus, plagiarism constitutes 'evils', 'misdoing', and 'a punishable wrong', invokes 'general loathing', 'fear', 'hate', and mistrust in teachers, and violates 'a tenet of a moral code'; plagiarising students are 'incorrigible by nature', 'psychopaths', 'cheaters', 'rascals', and 'villains' that teachers should 'hunt down' and 'righteously punish' (Kolich, 1983). Consequently, the moral discourse advocates monitoring the extent of student plagiarism, detecting its occurrence, catching its perpetrators, and adopting measures to effectively mitigate and deter it. In the words of Kolich (1983), 'like an avenging god I have tracked plagiarists with eagerness and intensity, faced them with dry indignation when I could prove their deception, and failed them with contempt' (p. 142). This detecting-and-punishing approach, however, may not be enough to deter student plagiarism (Duggan, 2006; East, 2009; Pecorari, 2013).

On the other hand, plagiarism is also seen as 'a legal minefield', because cases involving plagiarism may end up in courts (Park, 2003, p. 475). The legal perspective on plagiarism is tied to intellectual property and copyright laws (Park, 2003; Pennycook, 1996). From this perspective, plagiarism is considered to be theft or stealing of others' ideas or words. To quote Kolich (1983) again, 'the worm plagiarism spoils the fruit of intellectual inquiry and reason, and starves the seeds of originality that foster such inquiry' (p. 145). To nail plagiarism and punish the offender, the teacher or the institution concerned needs to come up with clear proof of plagiarism. However, as noted in Section 2.1, it is often difficult to establish the intent of the 'perpetrator' (Pecorari, 2001; Sutherland-Smith, 2005). As Kolich reminds us, 'the cut-and-paste paper or the paraphrased essay offers nothing conclusive about unworthy intentions and a corrupt heart' (Kolich, 1983, p. 147). On top of that, as evidenced in the literature, textual plagiarism may not necessarily involve the intent to deceive or to steal (Howard, 1999; Pecorari, 2003; Pennycook, 1996; Scollon, 1995). Thus, this perspective on plagiarism might be problematic as well.

The moral discourse on plagiarism has originated from the social mores, societal values, and dominant conceptions of morality that prevailed at the time of its inception. It is nourished by common perceptions of how plagiarism relates to and affects a teacher's and, by extension, an institution's work. Often, plagiarism is seen as challenging the reputation of a teacher/institution as an effective provider of quality education. As Kolich (1983) confides, 'I have always responded to plagiarism as a personal insult against me and my teaching' (p. 143). When operationalised in practice, the moral discourse requires the provision of objective textual evidence of plagiarism before appropriate punishments of offences are meted out (Sun & Hu, 2024). Such evidence is expected to come from teachers' eagle eyes in the old days and, more recently, various text-matching software (Hu, 2015b). This is why Turnitin and other similar detection programs were initially used as policing devices when they first came on the scene.

However, the moral discourse, when implemented, can victimise students who are not intent to deceive but lack the knowledge and skills to engage in institutionally or disciplinarily sanctioned intertextual practices (Yang et al., 2023). Thus, instead of treating it as misconduct or dishonesty, some scholars have been increasingly inclined to see plagiarism as poor practice or a developmental issue (Howard, 1999; Hu & Lei, 2015; Valentine, 2006). Ashworth et al. (1997, p. 200), for example, perceive plagiarism to be a breach of 'academic etiquette and polite behaviour'. Howard (1999) views patchwriting as an ineffective use of sources and a necessary developmental strategy. Additionally, it has been shown that definitions of plagiarism and institutional policies on plagiarism tend to focus on textual practices and disregard the authors and their intentions (Howard, 2000; Pecorari, 2001). As noted in Section 2.1 and earlier in this section, even when the author's intention is taken into account, it is often inferred from textual features rather than revealed by the author (Howard, 1999, 2000). As such, it is unfair and illogical to construe student plagiarists as being 'either unethical or ignorant of citation conventions', because 'attribution of ethics (or a lack thereof) personalises plagiarism, attaching it not to texts but to individuals' (Howard, 2000, p. 486). To debunk the confusion, Howard (2000) calls for 'more specific, less culturally burdened terms: fraud, insufficient citation, and excessive repetition' (p. 475) and goes so far as to argue for the removal of patchwriting from the juridical category of plagiarism. This and similar quests for morally neutral terms, as pointed out by Pecorari and Petrić (2014), 'shift the emphasis from crime and moral transgression to textual relations' (p. 279). As a result, the moral discourse is increasingly on the way out (Kaposi & Dell, 2012).

2.3 The Regulatory Discourse

The regulatory discourse, or what Kaposi and Dell (2012, p. 820) refer to as 'the discourse of proceduralism', characterises student plagiarism as a breach of academic rules or conventions rather than a transgression of moral principles (Adam et al., 2017; Kaposi & Dell, 2012). Drawing on a vocabulary of academic conventions, administrative guidelines and institutional rules, this discourse tends to depict plagiarism 'as inappropriate and unacceptable behaviour' rather than a crime (Park, 2004, p. 294) or a transgression of academic conventions rather than morality (East, 2010). Thus, according to the regulatory discourse, plagiarism can be either intentional or unintentional (Adam et al., 2017). The regulatory discourse includes plagiarism in institutional rules and regulations and stresses the importance of clear definitions and transparent guidelines regarding it (Kaposi & Dell, 2012; Park, 2004). Unlike the moral discourse that assumes students' natural awareness of legitimate source use, the regulatory discourse highlights the importance of clearly communicating rules and regulations on legitimate and illegitimate source use to students (Brown & Howell, 2001; Hu & Sun, 2017). In essence, the regulatory discourse underscores the importance of providing ethics education and promoting a culture of academic integrity to address plagiarism (Hu, 2015b; McCabe, 2001).

The regulatory discourse underlines institutional roles in defining illegitimate writing practices and disseminating transparent guidelines on espoused conventions. Thus, the literature has pointed to the need to develop institutional policies on plagiarism and other academic misconduct (Adam et al., 2017; East, 2010). An institutional policy typically highlights its endorsement of academic integrity and defines various forms of academic misconduct, including plagiarism (Sun & Hu, 2024). It may also specify faculty and student responsibilities to adhere to the policy (East, 2009). Furthermore, the regulatory discourse underscores the necessity of monitoring and regulating strict adherence to the valorised academic tradition/practices through institutional policies and ethics education of students. Institutional rules and regulations on plagiarism may include guidelines about source-use practices (including paraphrasing, summarising, quoting, in-text citation, and referencing) and examples of legitimate and illegitimate source use, which are expected to guide students to avoid plagiarism (Adam et al., 2017). They may also 'set the parameters for reporting, investigating and penalising infringements' (Gullifer & Tyson, 2014, p. 1203). This discourse usually places the onus of responsibility not only on institutions but also on students to self-regulate their behaviours and abide by the rules and regulations governing plagiarism (Hu, 2015a, 2015b). McCabe (2005b), for example, stresses the need to 'develop students who accept responsibility for the ethical consequences of their ideas and actions' (p. 29).

However, research on actual institutional policies has revealed a lack of clear conceptualisations of plagiarism (Adam et al., 2017; Eaton, 2017; Hu & Sun, 2017; Merkel, 2021). For example, Sutherland-Smith (2008) examined university policies on plagiarism in Australia, Canada, China, England, New Zealand, and the USA, and found that definitions of plagiarism involve different levels and types of plagiaristic practices. Similarly, Sun and Hu's (2024) analysis of the institutional policies on plagiarism issued by eight universities in Chinese Mainland and eight universities in Hong Kong reveals considerable inter-institutional disagreement and inconsistency in the communication of information on plagiarism, the mechanisms for detecting plagiarism, the academic guidance and support provided for avoiding plagiarism, and the specific approaches taken to address the problem. Moreover, the advent and use of ChatGPT and other large language models that can generate academic texts have drawn wide discussion (Nature, 2023; Stokel-Walker, 2023) and posed challenges for the formulation of institutional policies underpinned by the regulatory discourse. For example, whereas some universities allow students to submit texts generated by large language models provided they acknowledge the use of these AI tools and/or explain how the tools are used, others explicitly prohibit the use of such tools in assignments (Lund et al., 2023). The rapid development of and wide access to generative AI make it ever more challenging for institutions to come up with effective rules and guidelines on plagiarism.

Furthermore, the effectiveness of institutional guidelines in eliminating or reducing plagiarism has been called into question. For one thing, most of these guidelines are too general to be readily applicable for students (Devlin, 2006; Eaton, 2017). Thus, students tend to grapple with what constitutes various forms of plagiarism, especially more subtle ones, and how to avoid them

(Bretag et al., 2014; Gullifer & Tyson, 2010). For another thing, even when provided with the guidelines, students may not read them (Gullifer & Tyson, 2014; Power, 2009). In a critical analysis of one American university's multiple plagiarism policies, Merkel (2021) found that the policies were dominated by discourses of authority and ethics and that it was confusing and problematic for students to relate the policies to their individual disciplines. In this regard, students have reported being unsure about the rules of source use (Brimble & Stevenson-Clarke, 2005; Devlin & Gray, 2007; Hu & Lei, 2015) and unable to identify plagiarised texts in writing samples (Chandrasegaran, 2000; Deckert, 1993; Hu & Lei, 2012; Wheeler, 2009). Hence, it is recommended that 'deterrence and proactive strategies both should play an important role in any academic integrity policy' (McCabe, 2005b, p. 31). Such proactive strategies should be pedagogical in nature and informed by a developmental perspective on students' acquisition of intertextual skills.

2.4 The Developmental Discourse

There is a growing recognition of textual borrowing as a learning or developmental issue rather than a moral or self-regulatory issue (Flowerdew & Li, 2007b; Howard, 1999; Pecorari, 2023; Pecorari & Petrić, 2014). Howard (1999), for example, identifies such an intertextual practice as 'something that all academic writers do' (p. xviii). This recognition of textual appropriation, including transgressive intertextual practices, as integral to students' academic writing development has given rise to a developmental discourse on plagiarism. As Hu and Sun (2017, pp. 58–59) summarise, the developmental discourse

> recognizes plagiarism as a concept that is not readily susceptible to an unambiguous universal definition, academic writing as a social practice that involves negotiations of authorial intentions and identities, and students as developing academic writers who need educative support in their immersion in and acquisition of academic literacy.

It is difficult to chalk up a universal definition of student plagiarism partly because the literature has identified a multitude of reasons for L2 students' inappropriate source use, including unfamiliarity with the Western notion of plagiarism (Pennycook, 1996; Scollon, 1995; Shi, 2006), limited L2 language proficiency (Hayes & Introna, 2005a; Keck, 2006; Plakans & Gebril, 2012), restricted experiences with or skills in source-based writing (Abasi & Akbari, 2008; Angélil-Carter, 2000; Rinnert & Kobayashi, 2005), lack of training in plagiarism (Sun & Hu, 2020; Yang et al., 2023), among others. Scollon (1995) rightly points out that 'the concept of plagiarism is fully embedded within a social, political, and cultural matrix that cannot be meaningfully separated from its interpretation' (p. 23). Similarly, Chandrasoma et al. (2004) observe that transgressive intertextuality is concerned not only with textual practices but also with 'intentionality, development, identity, resistance, student epistemologies, common knowledge, mediated discourse, interdisciplinarity, variability, and task type' (p. 188). This growing recognition of the complexity of plagiarism has paved the way for a developmental view of transgressive intertextuality.

The developmental discourse sees intertextuality, including patchwriting, as a social practice that involves negotiations of authorial intentions and identities. It has been shown that patchwriting is a transitional stage and a developmental strategy for all learners (Campbell, 1990; Howard, 1999; Pecorari, 2003; Roig, 2001). Angélil-Carter (2000), for example, posits that plagiarism in student writing is more of an issue of academic literacy than 'intentional "dishonesty", "theft" or "immorality"' (p. 61). In line with the developmental discourse on plagiarism, Howard (1999) argues that 'patchwriting has a legitimate and valuable place in literacy instruction' (p. xxii). She goes on to call for taking into account authorial intentions 'in determining what is and is not plagiarism' (Howard, 1999, p. xxii). Accordingly, 'patchwriting qualif[ies] as plagiarism and thus as transgression only if the author's intention is fraudulent—only if the author, the student, appears to have been trying to deceive his or her readers' (Howard, 1999, p. xxii). Without evidence of intentional deception, patchwriting should be regarded as learning rather than cheating by default. As Pecorari and Petrić (2014) note, although this view has been taken up by an increasing number of L2 writing researchers, it has not gained much traction with L2 writing instructors or researchers in other disciplines.

Apart from authorial intentions, patchwriting also involves negotiation of authorial identities. Extant research (e.g., Hirvela & Du, 2013; Shi, 2010) has revealed that student writers may regurgitate words from sources in order to establish an authorial voice. In a study of students' self-reflections on their textual appropriation practices, Shi (2010) identified a tension between 'a reliance on source texts for support and an attempt to establish their own voice by choosing not to cite' (p. 21). Students under pressure to project an authorial voice beyond their reach may see textual borrowing as a resource (Pecorari & Petrić, 2014). In addition, L2 students may choose to appropriate source texts to mask their novice and/or L2 identities (Abasi et al., 2006; Shi, 2006; Starfield, 2002). Abasi et al. (2006), for example, found that less experienced L2 academic writers had a weaker sense of authorial identities and were more likely to copy from sources compared with more experienced L2 academic writers. There is thus a need to 'recogniz[e] plagiarism as part of literacy practices governing identity construction' (Ouellette, 2008, p. 255) and 'foster a sense of meaning, empowerment, and clarity in students' for source-using practices (Moss et al., 2018, p. 274).

Finally, the developmental discourse views students as developing academic writers who may go through plagiarism as a developmental stage. As an integral part of academic writing, textual borrowing or patchwriting is closely intertwined with students' developing academic writing skills (Howard, 1995; Luzón, 2015). Reviews of extant research on plagiarism and second language writing have pointed to textual borrowing as an integral part of language learning and writing development (Flowerdew & Li, 2007b; Pecorari & Petrić, 2014). In a longitudinal study of ten Chinese students transitioning to the UK higher educational system, Gu and Brooks (2008) observed that 'rather than being an act of cheating, patchwriting is a learning strategy that students use to engage with the linguistic and discursive forms of their disciplines' (p. 347). In another study of the knowledge of plagiarism and the ability to recognise plagiarism among university students in Rwanda, Clarke et al. (2023) showed that master's students had greater knowledge about plagiarism and better ability to recognise it than students at the diploma or bachelor levels. They attributed the master's students' better understanding and detection of plagiarism to their more exposure to writing and reading in disciplinary literacy practices. Thus, patchwriting can be characterised as 'a form of textual plagiarism which is caused not by the intention to deceive but by the need for further growth as a writer' (Pecorari, 2003, p. 338). In a similar vein, Petrić (2012) found that more advanced L2 students made an excessive use of quotations in their academic writing to mark their intertextual appropriations and show their awareness of legitimate and unacceptable intertextual practices.

In summary, the moral discourse views plagiarism as intentional, dishonest, immoral, and reprehensible, and consequently advocates for the monitoring and detection of student plagiarism, the ensnaring of offending individuals, and the implementation of disciplinary measures to reduce and prevent it. The regulatory discourse characterises student plagiarism as a violation of academic rules rather than a transgression of moral principles, emphasises the institutional role in defining illegitimate writing practices and disseminating transparent rules on established norms, and underscores the need to regulate rigorous adherence to the academic conventions through institutional policies and ethics education. The developmental discourse recognises plagiarism as defying a universal definition, academic writing as a social practice that involves negotiations of authorial intentions and identities, and students as developing academic writers who may go through plagiarism as a developmental stage. These discourses highlight the complexity of plagiarism as a concept and practice.

The complexity of plagiarism is also manifested to varying degrees in L2 students' perceptions of and stances on plagiarism, which are discussed in the next section.

3 L2 Students' Perceptions and Stances

A large body of research has examined L2 students' perceptions of and stances on plagiarism. This line of research has investigated a wide range of issues, including their perceptions of what constitutes plagiarism, their perceived causes of plagiarism, and their attitudes towards plagiarism, among others (see Cumming et al., 2016; Flowerdew & Li, 2007b; Liu et al., 2016; Pecorari & Petrić, 2014). With regard to L2 students' knowledge of plagiarism, there is considerable empirical evidence that L2 students tend to lack a sophisticated understanding of what constitutes plagiarism, especially more subtle forms of plagiarism (Hu & Lei, 2012; Wheeler, 2009). Some students may have no idea of what plagiarism is at all, whereas others may have a declarative knowledge of what plagiarism is but are unable to detect subtle plagiaristic practices (e.g., unacknowledged paraphrasing, patchwriting). As for stances on plagiarism, L2 students are perceived to hold lax attitudes towards plagiarism and be prone to committing plagiarism (Sapp, 2002; Sowden, 2005). This section unpacks L2 students' perceptions of and stances on plagiarism and disentangles the often-neglected connections between their perceptions and stances. It also critically assesses how and why L2 students' stances on plagiarism may be conflated with their knowledge of plagiarism in the extant literature and argues that L2 students' perceived lenient attitudes towards plagiarism might stem from their different conceptions of plagiarism.

3.1 L2 Students' Perceptions of Plagiarism

The literature has long acknowledged the importance of understanding students' perceptions of plagiarism and the need for teachers to be cognizant of students' perceptions (Howard, 1995; Rinnert & Kobayashi, 2005). As noted by Howard (1995), two of the most frequently mentioned causes of student plagiarism are 'an absence of ethics or an ignorance of citation conventions' (p. 788). In a survey of Iranian EFL (English as a Foreign Language) master's students' perceptions of different forms of plagiarism, Zafarghandi et al. (2012) found that lax attitudes towards and limited knowledge of plagiaristic behaviours were nominated as major contributors to student plagiarism. Similarly, Hu and Lei (2015) elicited perceptions of the likely causes of plagiarism from 270 undergraduate students at two Chinese universities and found that slack attitudes and inadequate academic ability were perceived to be the most likely inducements for student plagiarism. Shen and Hu (2021) administered the same survey instrument adopted in Hu and Lei (2015) to 183 master's students from three broad disciplinary groups at a major university in China, again finding that slack attitudes and inadequate academic ability were rated as the top two likely causes of plagiarism. Another cause rated highly likely by the participants was academic pressure (e.g., trepidation for failing a course and pressure to obtain good grades).

L2 students, especially those in or from Asia, have been reported to view what is and is not plagiarism (i.e., perceptions or knowledge of plagiarism) differently from Anglo-American academia due to the absence of the concept of plagiarism in their cultures and/or their limited exposure to the Anglo-American understanding of plagiarism. In particular, they have been found to have little awareness of the Western conception of plagiarism or understand it differently from the Western academic world (Amiri & Razmjoo, 2016; Rinnert & Kobayashi, 2005). In a survey of 211 first- and third-year students at a Hong Kong university, Deckert (1993) found that the participants 'had little familiarity with the Western notion of plagiarism and poor ability to recognize it' (p. 131). Similarly, in a study of Japanese university students' understandings of plagiarism, Rinnert and Kobayashi (2005) found that the participating students were less aware of citation conventions compared with their American counterparts. The study also found that students from the humanities and social sciences (HSS) were more aware of plagiarism than their peers from the sciences. The HSS students' greater awareness of plagiarism was attributed to their more experience with source-based writing and their teachers' greater concern about their source use. Also in the Asian educational context, Amiri and Razmjoo (2016) conducted semi-structured interviews with twelve Iranian EFL undergraduate students to investigate their perceptions of plagiarism, which revealed that the students had only a shallow understanding of plagiarism and tended to have difficulty in differentiating different forms of plagiarism.

Likewise, studies examining L2 students' abilities to detect inappropriate source use in textual examples have revealed their limited competence in identifying plagiaristic practices, including blatant ones (Chandrasegaran, 2000; Chien, 2017; Deckert, 1993; Hu & Lei, 2012; Wheeler, 2009). In a study of Chinese university students' abilities to recognise two types of plagiarism (i.e., unacknowledged copying and unattributed paraphrasing) in English writing samples, Hu and Lei (2012) found that only slightly over one-third of the students identified unacknowledged verbatim copying as plagiarism, whereas less than 12 per cent of the students recognised unacknowledged paraphrasing as plagiarism. Drawing on a source-based writing task and interviews with sixty Taiwanese college students, Chien (2017) found that although the students seemed to be aware of the Western concept of plagiarism, their abilities to identify plagiarism were limited and that their source-use behaviours were not consistent with their understanding of plagiarism. Similarly, Clarke et al. (2023) found that although over three-fourths of the 330 Rwandan students in their study had a high level of knowledge of plagiarism, less than 12 per cent of them demonstrated a correspondingly high ability to recognise plagiaristic texts. Such findings point to the large discrepancies between 'knowing the principles of plagiarism and applying them' (Clarke et al., 2023, p. 258) and the need to distinguish declarative knowledge and procedural competence regarding plagiarism.

Furthermore, research comparing L1 and L2 students' perceptions of plagiarism has revealed substantial differences in their interpretations (Hayes & Introna, 2005a; Kayaoğlu et al., 2016; Marshall & Garry, 2006; Maxwell et al., 2008; Rinnert & Kobayashi, 2005; Shi, 2004, 2006). Marshall and Garry (2006) asked L1 and L2 students in New Zealand to judge whether provided scenarios involved plagiarism and, if so, how serious they found the identified instances of plagiarism to be. The study demonstrated that although both L1 and L2 students had problems understanding the concept of plagiarism and identifying plagiarism in the scenarios, L2 students fared worse than L1 students did. In another study of Turkish, Georgian, and German students' perceptions of plagiarism, Kayaoğlu et al. (2016) found that the German students were more capable of identifying plagiarism in sample texts than their Turkish and Georgian peers were, though large proportions of students in all three groups often failed to recognise some instances of plagiarism. The German students' greater sensitivity to plagiarism was attributed to the impact that the media coverage of several high-profile plagiarism scandals appeared to have on their perceptions. In an interview-based study of the perceptions of plagiarism among students from different cultural and linguistic backgrounds, Shi (2006) found that while students from China, Japan, and Korea tended to see plagiarism as both language and cultural problems, their peers from Germany were inclined to see it as a language problem. Overall, this research shows that L1 students tend to be more aware of plagiarism and its various manifestations and be more able to identify plagiaristic practices compared with L2 students.

3.2 L2 Students' Stances on Plagiarism

As regards L2 students' attitudes towards plagiarism, research has yielded mixed findings. Some studies (e.g., Ehrich et al., 2016; Yeo, 2007) have found L2 students to be lenient towards and even accepting of plagiarism, whereas others (e.g., Hu & Lei, 2012; Wheeler, 2009) have raised questions about the possibility of confounding knowledge of and stances on plagiarism in previous research. In general, earlier studies were more likely to report L2 students holding lax attitudes towards plagiarism and being prone to committing plagiarism. In a study of Japanese university students' understandings of plagiarism, for example, Rinnert and Kobayashi (2005) found that Japanese university students tended to hold an ambivalent attitude towards unacknowledged borrowing of others' ideas or words. Similarly, in an investigation of first-year undergraduate science and engineering students' understandings of plagiarism at a large, multi-campus Australian university, Yeo (2007) found L2 students to favour more lenient penalties for plagiarism than their L1 counterparts did. Likewise, in a comparative study of Australian and Chinese undergraduate students' stances on plagiarism, Ehrich et al. (2016) revealed that the Australian students found using others' work less acceptable and held more negative attitudes towards plagiarism than the Chinese students did. The reported lax attitudes of L2 students were often ascribed to their moral deficiency and/or the absence of the concept of plagiarism in their culture (Sowden, 2005). Rinnert and Kobayashi (2005), for example, linked their Japanese students' ambivalent attitudes to education and literacy practices (e.g., limited prior experience with source-based writing, lack of instruction on source use in L1), as well as an inadequate understanding of the concept of plagiarism and the absence of strict policies on plagiarism in student writing.

More recent studies tended to paint a more complex picture with respect to L2 students' stances on plagiarism. Some of these studies (e.g., Hu & Lei, 2012; Wheeler, 2009) tried to address a limitation of previous work, that is, a failure to tease apart L2 students' knowledge of and attitudes towards plagiarism. Thus, it was not clear whether L2 students' greater tolerance of different forms of plagiarism was due to their ignorance of such plagiaristic practices, their different understandings of what is and is not plagiarism, or other non-knowledge factors. Yang et al. (2023) argue that 'students' perceptions of plagiarism (e.g., its causes and acceptability) and attitudes toward it reflect their understanding of what constitutes legitimate intertextual practices, including appropriate paraphrasing' (p. 659). In other words, L2 students may define what is and is not plagiarism differently from the Western concept of plagiarism. As such, it is not surprising that L2 students are found to be lenient towards what they do not consider to be plagiarism. This view is supported by the findings of several studies.

Hu and Lei (2012), for example, investigated Chinese university students' abilities to recognise two forms of plagiarism (unacknowledged copying and paraphrasing) in English writing samples, their stances on the identified plagiarism, as well as factors influencing their abilities to detect the two forms of plagiarism. The study showed that the great majority of the students had difficulty in recognising the two forms of plagiarism, particularly unacknowledged paraphrasing. However, students held clearly punitive attitudes towards what they did identify as plagiarism. The study also found students' disciplinary background, self-reported competence in referencing, and knowledge of subtle plagiarism to be significant predictors of their abilities to detect both forms of plagiarism. In light of these findings, previously reported lax attitudes held by L2 students towards some plagiaristic practices may have emanated from their different perceptions/definitions of plagiarism. These findings point to the necessity and importance of differentiating students' knowledge of and attitudes towards plagiarism. In another study involving 212 English-major students from nine Chinese universities, Yang et al. (2023) also found that as a group, the participants gave low ratings (mostly below 2 on a 5-point Likert scale) of the acceptability of plagiarism caused by inadequate academic ability, slack attitudes, academic pressures, and perceived low risk of plagiarising. In addition, they held strong condemnatory attitudes towards plagiarism in general, as reflected in the mean rating of 4.44 on a 5-point Likert scale. Notably, the students were asked to complete a paraphrasing task, and their paraphrases were scored for verbatim copying from the source text. Yang et al. found that students with previous training in plagiarism, having knowledge of blatant plagiarism, and holding a punitive attitude towards plagiarism had significantly lower verbatim copying scores and paraphrased the source text more appropriately than their counterparts without such training, knowledge, or attitudes.

To shed light on the underlying causes of L2 students' attitudes, a number of studies have examined the relationship between L2 students' demographic variables and their knowledge of and stances on plagiarism (Hu & Lei, 2015; Quah et al., 2012; Yang et al., 2023). Hu and Lei (2015), for example, investigated the relationship between Chinese undergraduate students' demographic variables (gender, year of study, disciplinary background) and their knowledge of blatant and subtle plagiarism. Chen and Chou (2017) examined the relationship between students'/faculty's demographic variables (gender, academic level, disciplinary background) and their understandings of and stances on plagiarism. Both studies identified significant effects of academic level and disciplinary background on students' understandings of and attitudes towards plagiarism. However, whereas Hu and Lei (2015) found a non-significant effect of gender, Chen and Chou (2017) found that male and female participants differed markedly. In addition, Ehrich et al. (2016) examined the relationship between pressure and attitudes towards plagiarism and found that pressure felt by students was significantly associated with the severity of their attitudes towards plagiarism. In the aforementioned study by Yang et al., participating students' institutional contexts (i.e., top-tier universities versus ordinary ones) and English proficiency scores were found to be significant predictors of their abilities to paraphrase a source text legitimately. These findings suggest that a multitude of factors bear on students' knowledge of and stances on plagiarism. For this reason, 'it is likely that there is no single explanation for why individuals engage in plagiarist behaviors' (Ehrich et al., 2016, p. 232). The next section will discuss four sets of factors that may contribute to L2 students' illegitimate intertextual practices.

4 Factors Contributing to L2 Students' Plagiarism

It is crucial to explore factors contributing to L2 students' plagiarism because doing so can enhance and expand our understanding of plagiarism and strategies for curbing it effectively (Pecorari & Petrić, 2014). Research has shown that cultural traditions, L1 literacy practices, low language proficiency, and insufficient knowledge of and engagement in source-based writing are among the common factors that contribute to inappropriate L2 source use (Howard, 1999; Liu et al., 2016; McKenna, 2022; Scollon, 1995). In an interview-based study of twelve Iranian university students' perceptions of plagiarism, Amiri and Razmjoo (2016) identified a number of factors contributing to student plagiarism, including students' limited writing and research skills, instructors' indifference or neglect, peer pressure, pressure to submit high-quality assignments, and ease of plagiarising. Based on their thematic review and synthesis of fifty-three empirical studies on source use, Liu et al. (2016) point to cultural-historical (e.g., culture-specific literacy practices and strategies), cognitive (e.g., superficial cognitive processing of disciplinary subjects, lack of cognitive resources for skilled synthesis, and lack of critical thinking skills), and educational factors (e.g., lack of instruction on appropriate source use, faculty members' lax attitudes towards student plagiarism, and lack of training in critical reading) as contributors to or influencing factors of L2 student plagiarism.

In another review focusing on perceptions of, attitudes towards, and factors contributing to plagiarism, AL Harrasi (2023) examined sixty-one studies published from 1997 to 2016 and identified five sets of factors contributing to student plagiarism: institutional, academic, external, personal, and technological. First, the institutional factors include teaching strategies and methodology, conventional teaching methods/poor assessment methods (tests-oriented), and unclear policies on academic misconduct and related penalties. Second, the academic factors comprise the type, difficulty, and nature of tasks/assignments, subject matter, lack of understanding of the tasks/assignments, poor language (writing) skills, excessive demands for assignments, and large numbers of assignments. Third, the external factors consist of peer behaviours, cultural factors, peer pressure, and parental pressure. Fourth, the personal factors include students' lack of time, poor time management, laziness, unfamiliarity with the concept of plagiarism, perceptions of plagiarism, attitudes towards plagiarism, desire for better grades, and perceptions of lecturers' unawareness and disinterest regarding student plagiarism. Fifth, the technological factors involve easy access to materials on the Internet, ease of copying via the Internet and other technologies, and access to software programmes used for detecting plagiarism.

It is clear that a wide range of factors may contribute to plagiarism and these factors can be categorised into four clusters, namely the moral, cultural, practical, and developmental factors.

4.1 Moral Factors

Students' plagiaristic practices are typically attributed to moral deficiencies or lapses by default (Howard, 1999). One of the most frequently mentioned causes of student plagiarism is 'an absence of ethics' (Howard, 1995, p. 788), that is, a system of values concerning what is right or wrong. The literature has identified 'lack of a felt moral obligation to avoid cheating' as a possible contributor to plagiarism and other types of academic misconduct (Whitley, 1998, p. 259). There is, however, a need to differentiate intentional and unintentional plagiarism before ascribing plagiarism to students' moral deficiency or lapse. As noted in Section 2.2, although it makes sense to label intentional plagiarism as a moral lapse, there is a growing recognition that unintentional plagiarism should not be characterised as a moral transgression. An L2 student may commit plagiarism simply because he or she does not know that the intertextual practice in question is a form of plagiarism recognised as such by the L2 academic community. The distinction between intentional and unintentional plagiarism notwithstanding, institutional policies on plagiarism tend to view it as rooted in morals. Merkel (2021), for example, found that the plagiarism policies of nine colleges at the University of Iowa characterised plagiaristic behaviours as moral breaches that violated the university's core values and would lead to dire consequences. Similarly, Hu and Sun's (2017) analysis of eight Chinese universities' plagiarism policies revealed that most of these policy texts discussed plagiarism in moral terms and adopted a catch-and-punish approach. Even students themselves see plagiarism as a moral transgression. For example, a student in Shen and Hu (2021) asserted that 'I think plagiarism is an abominable act that speaks volumes about a person's moral standing/quality'

(p. 214), and another student characterised plagiarism as a 'deceptive behavior' linked to 'degraded personality and [being] hypocritical' (p. 214).

The literature has also suggested that perceived low likelihood of being caught and punished is likely to predispose some students to engage in plagiarism (Husain et al., 2017; Pecorari, 2013; Selwyn, 2008). For example, the undergraduate students ($N = 270$) in Hu and Lei (2015) gave a mean rating of 2.82/5 to low risks of being caught as a cause of plagiarism, though they rated the acceptability of such plagiarism low (i.e., 2.15/5). Similar but slightly lower ratings were obtained from the 183 master's students in Shen and Hu (2021). Perceived seriousness of plagiarism may also modulate students' proneness to plagiarism (AL Harrasi, 2023). For example, research (e.g., Ashworth et al., 1997; Maxwell et al., 2008) has shown that students who see plagiarism as a minor issue are more likely to plagiarise. Yang et al. (2023), on the other hand, reported that L2 students who found plagiarism unacceptable and deserving punishment were less likely to copy verbatim from a source text. Conversely, in a survey of Iranian EFL master's students' perceptions of different forms of plagiarism, Zafarghandi et al. (2012) found lax attitudes towards plagiarism a major contributor to student plagiarism. Similarly, in a survey study of 270 Chinese university students' perceptions of plagiarism, Hu and Lei (2015) found that almost 90 per cent of the participants reported slack attitudes as a possible or probable cause of Chinese university students' plagiarism.

Furthermore, peers' perceptions and practices of plagiarism may also have a bearing on students' propensity towards deceptive plagiarism. For example, peer disapproval of plagiarism tends to deter students from plagiarising, whereas peer approval of and engagement in plagiarism are likely to induce students to plagiarise (McCabe & Trevino, 1997; Sutton & Taylor, 2011). Ashworth et al. (1997) found an important role of peer-related values and ethics in student justifications of plagiarism, reporting that the master's students interviewed by them thought plagiarism was justifiable when it concerned friendship, peer trust, and interpersonal loyalty. In their review of empirical research, Husain et al. (2017) also revealed that peer behaviours, group dynamics, and peer pressure were found by some previous studies to be critical factors that could contribute to plagiarism. This points to the role of a normative structure that allows or disallows plagiarism in shaping students' proclivity to plagiarise (Whitley, 1998).

4.2 Cultural Factors

Cultural factors link L2 students' plagiarism to their cultural backgrounds, literacy practices, and/or educational traditions, which are believed to endorse different, if there are any, conceptions of plagiarism from those espoused in Anglo-American academia (Flowerdew & Li, 2007b; Pecorari, 2023; Pecorari & Petrić, 2014). As noted in Section 1, the cultural-conditioning view holds that different cultures may have different conceptualisations of plagiarism and some cultures may not have such a concept as plagiarism (Liu, 2005; Phan, 2006; Sowden, 2005). Students from some cultures may find the concept of plagiarism alien (Pennycook, 1996; Sowden, 2005) and even resist it (Currie, 1998; Pennycook, 1996). The perceived proclivity to plagiarise among L2 students is then often attributed to the absence of the concept of plagiarism and associated notions in their cultures (Matalene, 1985; Sowden, 2005), such as authorship, ownership, and intellectual property, which are rooted in the Western culture and may not be shared by other cultures (Chandrasoma et al., 2004; Howard, 1995; Pennycook, 1996; Scollon, 1995).

However, some scholars (e.g., Matalene, 1985; Pennycook, 1996) have cast doubt on the legitimacy of imposing the Western concept of plagiarism and its underlying values and norms on other cultures. For one thing, researchers (e.g., Lundsford, 1999; Rinnert & Kobayashi, 2005) have called into question the notion of individual ownership of texts. For another, there is evidence showing that plagiarism has always been condemned in Chinese history (Li, 2024), and there are two words (*piaoqie* and *chaoxi*) expressing the idea of plagiarism in Chinese (see Li & Flowerdew, 2018; Liu, 2005). It has been shown that the lack or inadequacy of training in intertextual practices in Chinese literacy practices and China's educational system may largely account for Chinese students' conceptual confusion about and perceived proneness to plagiarism (Hu & Lei, 2012; Li & Flowerdew, 2018).

In addition to cultural backgrounds, literacy practices endorsed in some cultures may also contribute to L2 students' plagiarism (Matalene, 1985; Pennycook, 1996). The literature has linked L2 students' plagiarism to memorisation and regurgitation of texts in their L1 literacy practices, and copying and imitating in their L1 as well as L2 learning experiences (Chandrasoma et al., 2004; Scollon, 1995). Specifically, memorising and regurgitating texts are common literacy practices in some cultures, such as Chinese, Vietnamese, Italian, Japanese, and Singaporean cultures (Chandrasegaran, 2000; Dryden, 1999; Matalene, 1985; Sapp, 2002; Sherman, 1992). For example, the Italian university students in Sherman's (1992) study were found proud of reproducing memorised texts from textbooks in exams. In a similar vein, the Singaporean students in Chandrasegaran's (2000) study were found to value the regurgitation of source information though they would probably do so in their own words. Likewise, the Chinese students in Sapp's (2002) study valorised the practice of memorising and recalling knowledge in preparing for exams. The Chinese students in Matalene's (1985) study were also found to have a fervour for memorising classical texts and reproducing them in their writings. In reference to such literacy practices, a participant in Sun and Hu (2020) observed that

> For freshmen and sophomores, the so-called 'plagiarism' is acceptable. Their English language proficiency is limited, and they cannot write good essays on their own. For these students, memorizing sample essays and using well-written sentences from these essays can make their writing better. This is a learning process and should be encouraged. (p. 469)

Thus, despite the association of memorisation and regurgitation with plagiarism, the literature has suggested that memorising and reproducing texts is a legitimate and even valorised literacy practice indicative of hard work (Hu & Lei, 2012; Liu, 2005; Matalene, 1985; Pennycook, 1996; Scollon, 1995). As Liu (2005) points out, 'a major role of memorizing good writing in Chinese is to help the learner to appreciate and become familiar with effective rhetorical styles and useful writing techniques that the memorized writing uses so the learner can use them in his/her own writing in the future' (p. 234). Such a view was also held by some Chinese university teachers in Sun and Hu (2020), who openly or tacitly encouraged their students to '"borrow sentences" from exemplary texts to embellish and sophisticate their own writing' (p. 469). Extant research (e.g., Matalene, 1985; Pennycook, 1996; Shi, 2006) has shown that imitating and repeating others' words is an integral part of L2 students' language learning and writing development. There is thus a need for 'reevaluating the scope and value of imitation as a legitimate form of authorship' (Howard, 2000, p. 487).

Educational practices embedded in specific sociocultural contexts may also have a role to play in L2 students' plagiarism (Liu et al., 2016). It has been suggested that some time-honoured educational practices, such as rote learning and exam-oriented assessment, tend to lead L2 students to plagiarise (Sapp, 2002; Sowden, 2005). Additionally, L2 students' lack of exposure to and training in legitimate source use may also contribute to their inappropriate source use (Bikowski & Gui, 2018; Hayes & Introna, 2005a; Rinnert & Kobayashi, 2005; Shi, 2006), which points to the key role of academic socialisation in fostering adequate knowledge of and appropriate attitudes towards plagiarism (AL Harrasi, 2023; Hu & Lei, 2016). As Hayes and Introna (2005a) observe, in some cultures (e.g., Asian, Chinese, Greek), university teaching centres on textbooks, and assessment often takes the form of exams, where students are required to recall what they have learned from the textbooks. As a result, L2 students from these cultures may not have had much experience with source-based writing and are therefore more likely to have problems with source use in their writing (Hu & Lei, 2012; Rinnert & Kobayashi, 2005). Rinnert and Kobayashi (2005), for example, attributed Japanese university students' unfamiliarity with citation conventions to their limited experience with source-based writing in high school, their restricted exposure to the notion of plagiarism, the lack of systematic training in L1 citation in Japanese universities, as well as the lack of strict institutional policies on plagiarism/*ukeuri* in student writing (also see Liu et al., 2016).

In sum, a multitude of cultural factors may contribute to L2 students' plagiarism. With regard to the relationship between culture and plagiarism, expressed opinions and empirical evidence are 'fragmented and contradictory' (Pecorari & Petrić, 2014, p. 286). Some researchers (e.g., Flowerdew & Li, 2007b; Hu & Lei, 2012; Wheeler, 2009) have highlighted the need to both acknowledge cultural differences and avoid cultural stereotyping. In particular, the cultural-conditioning view on plagiarism is likely to lead to the stereotyping of L2 students and the failure to provide support needed by L2 students to use sources effectively in their writing (Li & Flowerdew, 2018; Liu, 2005; Phan, 2006). Thus, while acknowledging cultural differences in the conceptualisations of plagiarism, Gu and Brooks (2008) caution against over-emphasising the role of cultural differences because doing so 'may result in a dismissive attitude towards Chinese learning practices' (p. 338). In response, Li and Flowerdew (2018) makes a useful suggestion about replacing the cultural-conditioning view with a cultural and historical development perspective on plagiarism to capture the 'dynamic and context-sensitive' (p. 151) nature of intertextual practices and their acquisition.

4.3 Practical Factors

Practical factors contributing to L2 students' plagiarism include pressure of various kinds, such as pressure to get a high grade, complete too many assignments within a tight timeline and survive a course, as well as various contextual influences such as faculty members' lax attitudes towards plagiarism, lack of actions regarding identified instances of plagiarism, and lack of clear institutional policies on plagiarism (Bowen & Nanni, 2021; Hayes & Introna, 2005a; McCabe et al., 2002; Selwyn, 2008; Tremayne & Curtis, 2021). In a review article of plagiarism by university students, Park (2003) identified a range of reasons for student plagiarism, including efficiency gain (e.g., to get a better grade or to save time), attitudes towards teachers and class (e.g., negative attitudes towards teachers, assignments, and tasks), time management, temptation, opportunity, and lack of deterrence, among others. Most of these reasons were corroborated by the findings of several studies conducted in the Chinese context. Across disciplines, undergraduate students in Hu and Lei (2015) and postgraduate students in Shen and Hu (2021) rated pressure of various kinds (e.g., to submit assignments on time, obtain good grades, survive competition among peers, and avoid flunking a course) a very likely cause of student plagiarism (i.e., 3.47/5 and 3.36–3.53/5, respectively). These ratings were consistent with the ratings on pressure as a likely cause of plagiarism reported in Lei and Hu's (2015) study of 112 Chinese university EFL teachers with and without overseas academic experience (i.e., 3.13/5 and 3.04/5, respectively).

Similar findings came up in studies conducted in other educational contexts. In an interview- and questionnaire-based study of international students studying in Australian universities, Song-Turner (2008) found time constraints, stress, and tensions involved in adapting to a new context, and a desire to respect the foreign experts and their words to be major contributors to their plagiaristic behaviours. Likewise, Comas-Forgas and Sureda-Negre (2010) examined Spanish university students' perspectives on the factors contributing to academic plagiarism and revealed three sets of factors, including students' beliefs, behaviours and pressure arising from increased workloads, instructors' teaching methods, attitudes as well as the characteristics of the subject they teach, and the increased ease of access to information brought by technologies. Similarly, the Turkish, Georgian, and German students in Kayaoğlu et al.'s (2016) study identified a number of contributors to their plagiarism, such as heavy homework loads, busy schedule, easy access to academic sources, perceived low risks of being caught, and unclear assignment instructions. Drawing on interviews with twelve Iranian university students, Amiri and Razmjoo (2016) also found that pressure to submit high-quality assignments, students' limited writing competence and research skills, and ease of plagiarising were commonly reported factors contributing to student plagiarism. Although these and other practical factors are no excuses for committing plagiarism, they pose real challenges to students and should be accorded due attention.

Systematic reviews of extant research revealed that several contextual characteristics were accountable for student plagiarism. Liu et al. (2016), for example, noted that faculty's lax attitudes towards the consequences of plagiarism as well as lack of sufficient guidelines in institutional policies on plagiarism, of consistent regulations in university education, of explicit instruction on source use, and of institutional monitoring over the filing of plagiarism cases were facilitators of student plagiarism. Husain et al. (2017) came to similar conclusions. While some of these characteristics (e.g., lax attitudes and lack of relevant instructional provision) may, as noted in the preceding section, have to do with cultural traditions, teachers' apparent indifference to or neglect of plagiarism cases and their lack of pedagogical attention to plagiarism are also very likely to stem from their limited knowledge and competence concerning illegitimate intertextual practices. Hu and Shen (2021) found that although sizeable proportions of 128 Chinese university teachers were able to detect plagiarising texts presented in a judgement task, only 38 (29.69 per cent) of the 110 teachers who completed a paraphrase task were able to produce a legitimate paraphrase. Hu and Sun (2016) asked 108 Chinese EFL teachers from 38 universities to complete the same plagiarism-judgement and paraphrasing tasks. As many as 44 (40.74 per cent) of the teachers failed to recognise a plagiaristic paragraph, and another 40.62 per cent of the teachers who completed the paraphrasing task failed to produce a paraphrase free of verbatim copying from the source text. Similarly, of the 117 Chinese university English lecturers in Lei and Hu (2014), only 80 (68.38 per cent) and 45 (38.46 per cent) were able to identify an instance of unacknowledged copying and an instance of unattributed paraphrasing as plagiaristic. In another study of 137 Chinese university EFL teachers (Hu & Lei, 2016), the percentages of successful detection of the same two types of plagiarism were 75.18 per cent and 44.53 per cent, respectively. In a qualitative interview-based study of thirteen university EFL lecturers, Sun and Hu (2020) found that most of the teachers gave definitions of plagiarism indicating misconceptions, held ambivalent attitudes towards plagiarism (as reflected in their notions of harmless copying and copying as a learning strategy), did not engage in teaching about plagiarism due to a perceived lack of resources to do so, saw text matching tools primarily as devices for catching and punishing plagiarism, and expressed dissatisfaction with their university's lack of commitment to preventing plagiarism.

4.4 Developmental Factors

L2 students' engagement in illegitimate intertextuality has been increasingly seen in the literature on plagiarism as a developmental or learning issue rather than a moral one or even a cultural one (Flowerdew & Li, 2007b; Pecorari & Petrić, 2014). The developmental or learning factors have to do with L2 students' unfamiliarity with the Western concept of plagiarism (Pennycook, 1996; Scollon, 1995; Shi, 2006), insufficient language competence (Keck, 2006; Plakans & Gebril, 2013; Sun, 2012), and limited experiences with or skills in source-based writing prevalent in Western academia (Abasi & Akbari, 2008; Angélil-Carter, 2000; Petrić, 2004). In their state-of-the-art review of the literature on plagiarism in second language writing, Pecorari and Petrić (2014) conclude that '[t]here is now ample evidence that students may plagiarise unintentionally, as a result of uncertainty about citing conventions, what constitutes common knowledge, or limited referencing skills and/or L2 resources' (p. 276). Empirical evidence of student plagiarism as a developmental issue came from studies demonstrating that L2 students' knowledge of, stance on, and competence to engage in appropriate intertextuality changed over time in response to instructional experience and exposure to the Western concept of plagiarism.

First, a growing number of studies have found that L2 students' knowledge of plagiarism changes with advancement in higher education, more exposure to Western academia, or disciplinary enculturation. In a study of 211 university students in Hong Kong, Deckert (1993) found that the third-year students were better able to recognise different forms of textual plagiarism than their first-year counterparts. Similarly, Chandrasegaran (2000) demonstrated that Singaporean university students' ability to recognise unacknowledged copying and unattributed paraphrasing as plagiaristic grew with greater exposure to higher education. Although they focused on teachers, the findings of two studies are relevant to the discussion here. Lei and Hu (2015) reported that Chinese university EFL teachers with overseas academic experience scored higher in their knowledge of blatant plagiarism, subtle plagiarism, and inappropriate referencing than their counterparts without such experience did. These results were corroborated by Hu and Lei's (2016) findings that overseas-trained Chinese university teachers of English were better able to recognise blatant and subtle plagiarism than their home-trained counterparts, who in turn outperformed university students. Such findings indicate that knowledge of plagiarism is positively related to exposure to and experience in English academic writing.

Similarly, Song-Turner (2008) found that with increasing immersion in the Australian educational context, the definitions of plagiarism held by international postgraduate students at an Australian university became closer to the Western view. Hu and Lei (2012) revealed that Chinese HSS students were more capable of recognising both blatant and subtle plagiarism than engineering students. Likewise, Hu and Lei (2015) reported that Chinese EFL students from soft disciplines had significantly greater knowledge of both blatant and subtle plagiarism. Similar findings came up in Shen and Hu's (2021) study of Chinese EFL postgraduate students at a top university in China, which found that students in HSS knew more about subtle plagiarism than their counterparts in medical sciences or science and engineering disciplines. In their study of Chinese medical and English language teachers' knowledge of different forms of plagiarism in English writing, Hu and Shen (2021) found that longer teaching experience was associated with greater knowledge and that the English language teachers knew more about plagiarism than their medical colleagues did.

Second, the aforementioned studies also indicated that L2 students' stance on plagiarism varied with experience of academic writing, training in acceptable intertextual practices, disciplinary enculturation, and knowledge of various forms of plagiarism. Chandrasegaran (2000) found second- and third-year students at a Singaporean university more likely to view unacknowledged copying and unattributed paraphrasing as unacceptable than first-year students. However, Hu and Lei (2015) observed contradictory patterns: the third-year students in their study were more lenient towards plagiarism caused by slack attitudes and plagiarism in general than their first-year counterparts probably due to the greater pressures on them to obtain good grades for securing postgraduate admissions or better jobs. Hu and Lei (2012) found that students who had knowledge of the forms of plagiarism in question were more negative about such intertextual practices. Similar results were found in a study of Chinese university EFL teachers (Lei & Hu, 2014). Two other studies (i.e., Hu & Lei, 2016; Hu & Shen, 2021) revealed that Chinese university teachers with overseas academic experience held a more punitive stance on illegitimate intertextual practices than their peers without such experience. As for disciplinary differences, Shen and Hu (2021) reported that HSS students were more lenient towards plagiarism caused by inadequate academic abilities and perceived low risks than medical and/or science and engineering students were. That stance on plagiarism is affected by demographic and contextual factors attests to the developmental nature of intertextual practices.

Third, previous studies also found that competence to engage in appropriate intertextuality grew over time or in response to relevant academic experience. For example, Keck (2014) found that ESL students' duration of academic studies in the US was related to their abilities to copy less from a source text and paraphrase more appropriately. Abasi et al. (2006) showed that some ESL graduate students were more capable of using appropriate intertextual practices than others due to their greater disciplinary enculturation. Yang et al. (2023) reported that Chinese EFL undergraduate and postgraduate students who had received training in plagiarism produced more acceptable paraphrases than their peers without such training. Hu and Shen (2021) demonstrated that Chinese university teachers of English were less likely to copy verbatim from a source text in their paraphrases than teachers of medical sciences and psychology. Chinese EFL teachers who had overseas academic experience were more competent in producing acceptable paraphrases than their counterparts who did not have such experience (Hu & Sun, 2016). Perhaps the most direct evidence of intertextual competence being amenable to development comes from a ten-week intervention conducted at an

Omani university (AL Harrasi, 2023). A comparative analysis of pre- and post-intervention source-based essays by the students detected markedly fewer intertextual issues in the post-intervention essays.

Finally, a sizeable body of research has documented that EFL/ESL learners tend to have difficulty in writing from sources due to their limited English proficiency (McDonough et al., 2014; Plakans & Gebril, 2012). McDonough et al. (2014), for example, revealed that Thai students with low English proficiency compensated their inadequate English proficiency in writing from sources by frequently copying short strings of words from the sources. Plakans and Gebril (2012) also showed that L2 students less proficient in English found it challenging to understand a source text and focus primarily on vocabulary and grammar in their writing, whereas their more proficient peers had less difficulty in comprehending the source text and tended to focus mostly on content, cohesion, and rhetoric in their writing. Similarly, Cumming et al. (2006) examined L2 students' writings on independent and integrated writing tasks and compared their source-use practices across high, mid, and low scoring bands. They found that students receiving high scores produced more coherent summaries and syntheses, whereas those receiving mid and low scores used fewer paraphrases and summaries but more verbatim phrases from sources. Yang et al. (2023) reported that English proficiency was the strongest predicator of Chinese EFL students' ability to paraphrase a source text appropriately. Compared with native English-speaking students, L2 students often face greater challenges in using and citing sources because of their lesser English proficiency (Ellery, 2008; Hayes & Introna, 2005a): L2 students tend to copy more from source texts (Keck, 2006) and are less likely to cite the sources (Shi, 2004).

5 Approaches to Dealing with Plagiarism

Institutional responses to student plagiarism are largely characterised by detection, containment, and punishment (Briggs, 2003; Howard, 1995; Price, 2002). Likewise, both researchers and practitioners are inclined to take a primarily problem-oriented approach to plagiarism in L2 writing (Pecorari, 2023; Wette, 2010). As observed by Wette (2010), the literature on plagiarism is 'more problem-oriented than solution- or practice-oriented' (p. 159). Thus, the most prominent way to respond to plagiarism is to contain or regulate it (Howard, 1995; Price, 2002), giving rise to a punitive and a self-regulatory or disciplinary approach, respectively. However, as noted earlier, one of the most important contributors to L2 student plagiarism is a lack of exposure to and/or training in source use to develop the necessary knowledge and skills for engaging in appropriate intertextual practices. Thus, various scholars (e.g., Howard et al., 2010; Liu et al., 2016; Pecorari, 2013) have stressed the need to provide pedagogical support of L2 students' learning about source use, that is, the adoption of an educative approach to plagiarism (Adam et al., 2017; AL Harrasi, 2023; Hu, 2015b).

5.1 The Punitive Approach

The punitive approach is grounded in the moral discourse on plagiarism and views detection and retribution as an effective means of deterring plagiarism. Arguably, this is the earliest and most simplistic approach to plagiarism that is underpinned by deterrence theories and treats plagiarism 'as a moral crime that must be caught and punished ruthlessly' (Hu, 2015b, p. 100). In other words, plagiarism is characterised as a deliberate moral transgression that results from moral lapses, absence of ethics, temptations to deceive, among others (AL Harrasi, 2023; Kolich, 1983; Sutherland-Smith, 2011). The practitioner-oriented literature has advocated for '*post facto* disciplinary responses of exposure and punishment' (Ellery, 2008, p. 507) in the belief that sanctions outweighing potential gains of engaging in plagiarism can deter students from committing plagiarism. Thus, widely endorsed in academia and enshrined in institutional policy documents, the punitive approach embraces reactive and controlling practices and utilises plagiarism detection tools to detect (and deter) student plagiarism (Adam et al., 2017; Hu & Sun, 2017; Pecorari, 2001; Sutherland-Smith, 2011).

Despite its intended deterrent effects and wide endorsement, however, its long-term effectiveness in deterring and reducing student plagiarism has not been adequately substantiated with evidence (AL Harrasi, 2023; Sutherland-Smith, 2014). Specifically, although it may be effective in mitigating or curtailing intentional plagiarism, the punitive approach may not be able to reduce unintentional plagiarism (Moss et al., 2018). It is unlikely to work when students are not afraid of being caught or do not have the necessary competence to engage in acceptable source use (Hu, 2015b). Nor is it likely to work in institutions where efficient detection and filing of plagiarism are absent (McCabe, 2001). Moreover, the punitive approach may prevent students from making use of patchwriting, a useful and valuable composing strategy that affords a pedagogical opportunity to facilitate rather than thwart students' writing development (Howard, 1995; Pecorari, 2013). Sutherland-Smith (2011) also observes that simply 'implementing anti-plagiarism software detection along with increasing penalties does not necessarily reduce plagiarism' (p. 135).

There is thus a need to critique and guard against unfair and authoritarian practices prevalent in the punitive approach to plagiarism (East, 2006; Leask, 2006). In particular, the literature has highlighted the need for institutions to develop transparent, coherent, and consistent frameworks for dealing with plagiarism (Liu et al., 2016; Park, 2003). In this regard, most higher educational institutions have put in place institutional policies to respond to plagiarism (Hu & Sun, 2017; Pecorari, 2013). Meanwhile, it has been widely acknowledged that plagiarism detection tools can only provide an overall assessment of the extent of similarities between the text and the sources and can thus by no means be used as the sole determinant of whether plagiarism has occurred (Stapleton, 2012; Sutherland-Smith & Carr, 2005). For this reason, caution needs to be exercised when relying on plagiarism detection tools to determine and justify punitive responses to plagiarism. Furthermore, punitive responses to plagiarism may vary greatly depending on its perceived seriousness, ranging from warning, marking down, to suspension and expulsion (Currie, 1998; East, 2006; Howard, 1995). It is thus not enough to simply have clear and transparent rules and regulations. It is equally important to implement them consistently (Glendinning, 2014; Park, 2003; Pecorari, 2013). Finally, it is also important to make it easy for instructors to apply punitive measures and ensure they feel that their efforts to follow the institutional process are appreciated (Pecorari, 2013; Sutherland-Smith, 2010).

5.2 The Disciplinary Approach

The disciplinary approach subscribes to the regulatory discourse on plagiarism and relies primarily on students' own commitment to academic honesty and self-accountability for avoiding plagiarism (AL Harrasi, 2023; McCabe et al., 2002). Although patchwriting has been increasingly recognised as a transitional stage that all writers go through, some people would still adopt a juridical approach to it, holding that lack of intent is no excuse for plagiarism (Howard, 1999). There is thus a pressing need to 'move beyond deterrence, detection, and punishment' (Bretag, 2013, p. 2) and to take a disciplinary or ethics education approach (Hu, 2015b). Unlike the punitive approach that is premised on fear of being caught and punished, the disciplinary approach focuses on cultivating a culture of academic integrity and developing a sense of academic honour in students (McCabe, 2001). This approach typically entails the use of honour codes, focuses on communicating academic integrity as a fundamental institutional value to students, and obligates them to hold themselves accountable for enforcing institutional ethics standards and avoiding plagiarism (McCabe et al., 2002).

To develop a culture of academic integrity and cultivate students' sense of academic integrity, it is crucial for both institutions and faculty to 'recognize and affirm academic integrity as a core institutional value' (McCabe, 2005b, p. 29). In this spirit, institutions would enforce codes of conduct, organise ethics education, and issue rules and regulations on legitimate source use. Specifically, universities may provide handbooks that spell out their institutional honour codes and rules regarding academic misconduct as well as legitimate source use (e.g., referencing styles and requirements) (McCabe et al., 2002). The ethics education following this approach centres on explicitly making students become aware of institutional regulations and rules of legitimate source use and encouraging them to develop a sense of academic integrity and take responsibility for their own actions. For this purpose, students could engage in discussions of these codes of conduct and rules of source use (Bretag, 2013). According to Sutherland-Smith (2011), conceptualising plagiarism from the perspective of ethical rights and accountability 'reflects societal notions of justice and offers an educationally sustainable alternative' (p. 135) to the aforementioned punitive approach. In practice, however, institutional policies on plagiarism often adopt a mixture of the two approaches (Sun & Hu, 2024).

Communicating rules and regulations on plagiarism to students and placing the onus of responsibility to uphold academic integrity on students are insufficient to combat or tackle plagiarism (Bretag et al., 2014; East, 2009). While the disciplinary approach may be useful and effective in developing students' sense of academic integrity and equipping students with rules and regulations about legitimate source use (Bretag & Mahmud, 2016; Morris & Carroll, 2016; Pecorari, 2013; Walker & White, 2014), it is likely to fall short for students wishing to uphold ethical standards but lacking an appropriate understanding of what constitutes illegitimate intertextuality. In other words, a sense of academic integrity and an awareness of generic rules and regulations on source use are not enough to help students interact with sources appropriately in their writing (Gullifer & Tyson, 2014). Therefore, the literature has pointed to the need for a holistic approach that aligns institutional policies, teaching practices, and pedagogical processes for tackling plagiarism (Devlin, 2006; Duggan, 2006; East, 2009; Macdonald & Carroll, 2006). This is the educative approach that will be detailed in what follows.

5.3 The Educative Approach

Although plagiarism is generally seen as a breach of academic ethics or a violation of academic rules and primarily addressed in a punitive and/or a disciplinary approach, there is a growing tendency for L2 writing research to treat it as an issue of development and approach it from an educative perspective (Pecorari & Petrić, 2014). Pecorari (2013), for example, underscores the need to distinguish 'a police-like response to plagiarism and a teacherly one' (p. 44). The educative approach is informed by the developmental discourse on plagiarism and puts a premium on enculturation, whereby engagement with others' language and ideas is taught as a situated and meaning-making literacy practice that varies across sociocultural and educational contexts. Drawing on their review of fifty-three empirical studies of L2 student plagiarism, Liu et al. (2016) proposed nine recommendations for L2 source-use pedagogy, which are meant to '(a) ensure transparency in definitions, guidelines, and expectations, (b) build source-use knowledge, and (c) engage L2 English writers in continuous practice and autonomous development of plagiarism avoidance' (p. 36). In particular, the approach pivots on teaching students 'a range of skills and strategies, including text comprehension strategies, effective note-taking, paraphrasing, summarising, quoting and synthesising from multiple source texts', and 'providing ample opportunities for practice in a supportive learning environment in which students are not accused of plagiarism for making errors in the process of learning' (Pecorari & Petrić, 2014, p. 288).

Institutional policies on plagiarism typically treat plagiarism in all forms as a violation of academic ethics in need of adjudication (Howard, 1995; Sutherland-Smith, 2005). These policies and the moral/disciplinary discourse undergirding them leave little room for pedagogical alternatives (Hu & Sun, 2017; Kaposi & Dell, 2012). Intended for addressing prototypical or deceptive plagiarism, for example, they are 'ill suited for dealing with patchwriting' (Pecorari, 2013, p. 54), a developmental or transitional stage that L2 students typically go through. As Scollon (1995) argues, it is vital to go beyond approaching plagiarism from a moral or a legal perspective and take a peda-gogical approach to it. There is thus a need for 'a parallel set of measures with a focus on teaching and learning, rather than detection and punishment' (Pecorari, 2013, p. 54). In order to allow for pedagogical alternatives, it is crucial to revise institutional policies on plagiarism (Howard, 1995; Hu & Sun, 2017). The revised policies should incorporate 'an enlarged range of definitions and motiv-ations for plagiarism, which in turn enlarges the range of acceptable responses' (Howard, 1995, p. 789).

As regards anti-plagiarism pedagogy, the literature has suggested combing awareness-raising and skills-instruction (Barks & Watts, 2001; Bloch, 2012; Pecorari, 2023). It has been suggested that awareness-raising should focus not only on what constitutes plagiarism but also on why and how to engage with sources (Angélil-Carter, 2000; Pecorari & Petrić, 2014; Petrić, 2007). Students may use sources for different rhetorical purposes, such as agreeing or disagree-ing with an idea, explaining or justifying an idea, and applying concepts or ideas to their own analysis (Petrić & Harwood, 2013). Specifically, they may quote directly from sources out of four sets of motivations, '(a) source-related motivations (e.g., vivid expression of an idea), (b) writers' own goals (e.g., stylistic variety), (c) external factors (e.g., lack of time), and (d) students' beliefs and fears (e.g., fear of plagiarism)' (Petrić, 2012, p. 102). Without a solid understanding of source use and its functions, L2 students may overcite (Abasi & Graves, 2008) or overquote (Hirvela & Du, 2013) sources in their source-based writing. Thus, institutions and teachers need to understand the complex and multifaceted nature of source use as well as the context involved in order to come up with effective awareness-raising activities and practices.

It has, however, been shown that awareness-raising alone is insufficient to help students write effectively from sources (Abasi & Graves, 2008; Wette, 2010; Zhang et al., 2024), because they also need to develop adequate source-use skills (Du, 2019; Howard et al., 2010; Tomaš, 2010). Instructors are thus urged to provide students with guided opportunities for practising source use in their writing (e.g., writing film reviews) (Hu & Lei, 2012; Rinnert & Kobayashi, 2005). For this purpose, instructors need to design meaningful assignments that engage students in integrating sources into their writing meaningfully rather than encourage them to cut and paste source texts without a sound understanding (Bloch, 2001; Buranen, 1999). More specifically, several strategies have been proposed to deal with or make the best use of patchwriting, including 'a free-wheeling pedagogy of imitation' that allows the appropriation of others' language to negotiate group membership (Hull & Rose, 1989) and structured collaborative summary-writing (Howard, 1993). As observed by Howard (1995), both recommendations 'are made not in order to "prevent" or "cure" patchwriting but to help students make maximum intellectual use of it and then move beyond it' (p. 796).

Relatedly, research (e.g., Sun, 2009; Thompson et al., 2013) has shown that students need continuous engagement in source-using skills (e.g., paraphrasing, summarising, synthesising, referencing, forming arguments with sources) in order to 'transition from surface-level patchwriting to thorough rewriting' (Sun, 2009, p. 405). Pecorari (2013), along with others (Ellery, 2008; Hayes & Introna, 2005a), have pointed out the limitations of teaching solely the declarative facts about source use and argued for a process-based skills development approach to dealing with student plagiarism. It is thus crucial to provide students with authentic source-use tasks, feedback, as well as opportunities to revise or rewrite their texts (Petrić, 2012; Wette, 2010), because 'acquiring attitudes, values, norms, beliefs and practices is an ongoing and long-term process' (Ellery, 2008, p. 514). Taking a process-oriented approach to source-use instruction could also harness the educational potential of plagiarism detection tools (Hayes & Introna, 2005b; Li & Casanave, 2012). The literature has revealed that anti-plagiarism software can serve both a punitive function and an educative one (Liu et al., 2016; McCulloch et al., 2022). Liu et al. (2016), for example, point out that 'detection via anti-plagiarism software should be replaced with appropriate educational design to guide students away from illegitimate source-based writing' (p. 50). Instead of using them for the sole purpose of detection, a process-oriented educative approach could empower instructors to use text matching tools to develop students' source-using knowledge and skills.

Furthermore, it is also important for instructors to understand and appreciate L2 cultural and educational conventions and practices, which may differ from those endorsed in Western academia (Hayes & Introna, 2005a; Matalene, 1985; Pennycook, 1996; Scollon, 1995). Howard (1995), for example, admonishes that 'faculty should be alert to the possibility that students may not be attributing sources or may be patchwriting because of their own cultural traditions' (p. 802). For this reason, researchers (e.g., Hu, 2015b; Liu et al., 2016) have pointed to the need to explicate cultural differences in citation norms and practices to L2 learners so that they can internalise such differences and avoid plagiaristic practices in their writing. Regarding instruction on appropriate intertextual practices in English academic writing, Gu and Brooks (2008, p. 338) point out 'the inadequacy of focusing on writing skills' as universal and highlight the importance of raising teachers' awareness about 'the differing meanings of plagiarism across cultures'. To that end, instructors are encouraged to learn about their students' literacy practices and thereby design activities for students to explore their own literacy practices and compare them with those of the target community (Hu & Lei, 2012; Rinnert & Kobayashi, 2005).

Thus, the literature has stressed the importance of developing context-sensitive understandings of plagiarism and providing specific intertextual examples to address student plagiarism (Angélil-Carter, 2000; Hu & Lei, 2012; Marshall & Garry, 2006; Pecorari & Shaw, 2012; Shi, 2012). In a three-year action research project, Du (2022) designed a critical-pragmatic pedagogy to address plagiarism in an English for academic purpose writing class in the Chinese context. The pedagogy involved both learning source-attribution conventions and critical engagement with those conventions. Results from students' source-attribution performance in actual source-based writing and a questionnaire eliciting students' responses to each activity demonstrated the effectiveness of the pedagogy. The positive result was ascribed primarily to the enabling role of the pedagogy in shifting students' perceptions of academic conventions as 'unbreakable shackles' to 'avenues for developing effective expression and critical insight' (p. 11). It is thus vital to provide opportunities for both instructors and students to engage in critical discussions about the multifaceted nature of plagiarism and the prevailing conventions of intertextuality. To that end, Du (2022) urges practitioners 'to draw upon students' social and L1 experiences as valid problem-posing resources, and even to encourage students to question academic norms' (p. 11). As we have pointed out elsewhere (i.e., Hu, 2015b), however, 'the educative approach can be expected to help L2 students who are genuinely interested in learning to use sources legitimately and effectively but will conceivably be ineffectual with students who are intent on plagiarism or accidentally plagiarize for one reason or another' (p. 101). In the end, a multi-pronged approach is needed that is punitive, disciplinary, or educative where appropriate.

In summary, despite the growing body of literature on how to address plagiarism, few studies have examined the effectiveness of the proposed approaches, practices, and activities in developing L2 students' source-use awareness, knowledge, and skills (Cumming et al., 2016; Liu et al., 2016; Pecorari, 2023). Considering the complex and multifaceted nature of student plagiarism, there is no approach that can deal with all types of student plagiarism (AL Harrasi, 2023) and 'there are only good measures to be taken' (Robillard & Howard, 2008, p. 2). The small body of research (e.g., Choi, 2012; Du, 2019, 2022; Ellery, 2008; Wette, 2021) on the effectiveness of plagiarism or source-use pedagogy has shown the overall effectiveness of such pedagogical interventions in improving students' declarative knowledge and procedural competences in source use, and reducing unacknowledged source use. However, this research has also revealed the process of learning source use as a gradual and protracted one (Ellery, 2008; Hayes & Introna, 2005a; Pecorari & Petrić, 2014). As Liu et al. (2016) conclude, 'with more practice supported by appropriate use of detection software, the apprentices of Western academia may gain plagiarism awareness, knowledge, and skills required of appropriate source use' (p. 50).

6 Conclusion

In view of the complex, multifaceted, and contextually embedded nature of plagiarism, it is imperative to adopt a situated and holistic perspective on student plagiarism that gives due attention to cultural, educational, and disciplinary contexts (Abasi et al., 2006; Chandrasoma et al., 2004; East, 2006; Leask, 2006; Pecorari, 2023). As Robillard and Howard (2008) argue, 'plagiarism must be pluralized if we are to ethically and productively apply our nuanced knowledges about writing to this form of authorship' (p. 3). It is thus important to reconceptualise plagiarism by taking into account its multifarious interpretations, divergent discourses on it, distinctions between L2 students' knowledge of and stances on plagiarism, as well as the multitude and inter-actions of factors contributing to it. In doing so, plagiarism is approached and understood as intertextual practices 'where intention, interpretation and the academic community are construed as social practices concerning the negoti-ation of various identities and values – those of students as well as those of academics' (Kaposi & Dell, 2012, p. 813). This reconceptualisation under-scores the need to diversify and situate our approaches and responses to plagiarism.

The success of the punitive, disciplinary, and educative approaches to pla-giarism as well as their permutations is likely to vary substantially for different students and institutional circumstances (AL Harrasi, 2023; Hu, 2015a). As clearly demonstrated by AL Harrasi (2023), 'each approach to plagiarism management may not work properly for all types of [intertextual] issues' (p. 1080). The punitive approach, for example, stands a better chance to succeed in situations where students are both capable of engaging in appropriate source use and afraid of being caught for plagiarism and where institutions and faculty are highly vigilant to plagiaristic behaviours. In a similar vein, the disciplinary approach is likely to be effective for students who value academic honesty and know how to avoid plagiarism, but ineffective for students who wish to follow ethical standards but lack an adequate understanding of what constitutes illegit-imate source use and engage in transgressive intertextuality inadvertently. Finally, the educative approach is likely to work well for L2 students who are truly interested in learning how to use sources effectively, but it is bound to have no effects on students who intend to plagiarise and have no interest in learning how to use sources effectively.

Institutions need to have clear regulations and policies on plagiarism that can ensure the effective detection and handling of student plagiarism. Pecorari (2013) identifies two key characteristics of a good policy on plagiarism: it embodies the institution's shared understanding of plagiarism, and it is specific enough to enable faculty to feel confident about applying it. Pecorari (2013) also notes that a good policy on plagiarism should act as both a carrot and a stick at the same time, spelling out what can be gained by following it and making clear what can be lost if it is breached. For their policies on plagiarism to work, institutions must provide their students with the necessary instruction and resources that they need to avoid plagiarism and engage in legitimate intertextuality (Devlin, 2006; Duggan, 2006). Moreover, institutions have the responsibility to provide their faculty with the training and support needed to recognise student plagiarism and make appropriate, disciplinary, and pedagogical responses (Pecorari, 2013; Sutherland-Smith, 2010). Effective pedagogical responses require institution-wide professional development in teaching source use (Lei & Hu, 2014; Tomaš, 2010). In summary, institutions need to take a holistic and multipronged approach to addressing plagiarism that both introduces well-informed policy changes and provides faculty and students with adequate resources and support to do their part.

To achieve these institutional and pedagogical goals effectively, further research on plagiarism is needed. A forward-looking research agenda proposed by Pecorari (2023) identifies a number of key priorities. These include the development of a comprehensive rubric that captures the complex relationships between student and source texts, large-scale empirical efforts to establish the extent of plagiarism in student writing, further investigations into the impact of cultural differences on intertextual practices in a wider range of contexts, a close-up examination of the relationship between students' receptive/product-ive language skills and source-use practices, and longitudinal research on patchwriting as an intertextual strategy and practice to identify its developmen-tal trajectories and benefits. To provide empirical evidence for the appropriate-ness and effectiveness, or lack thereof, of the punitive, disciplinary and educative approaches to plagiarism, we need more research on policy and pedagogical strategies for preventing student plagiarism. As we have pointed out elsewhere (Hu, 2015b, p. 101), further research needs to address the following questions:

- Which strategies or combinations of them are effective/ineffective for whom in what contexts? In other words, what student characteristics and contextual variables mediate the effectiveness of the strategies in question?
- How does the efficacy of specific strategies interact with L2 students' socio-cultural and ethnolinguistic backgrounds?
- How do the promoted strategies engage disciplinary and paradigmatic epis-temologies and rhetorical conventions?
- How can the strategies promoted/recommended accommodate students' indi-vidual differences (e.g., motivation, moral understanding, L2 proficiency)?
- How can these strategies be effectively adapted to different genres, tasks, and communication contexts?
- What factors facilitate/inhibit L2 students' efforts to learn, adapt, or resist specific strategies?
- What kinds of ideologies undergird the strategies investigated?
- What other strategies or practices are in tension with the promoted ones?
- What resources (e.g., corpora, information and communication technology) can be drawn on effectively to support proven pedagogy?
- How can assessment practices be aligned to support promising strategies?

(Hu, 2015b, p. 101)

To conclude, this Element calls for a reconceptualisation of plagiarism as a complex, historically embedded, and context-sensitive practice and recommends a multipronged and concerted approach to dealing with plagiarism in second language writing that integrates useful elements from the punitive, disciplinary/self-regulatory, and educative approaches. This new approach aims not only to foster an ethical attitude towards plagiarism through education but also to develop L2 students' knowledge of various forms of plagiarism and their academic literacy skills in legitimate source use through focused pedagogical activities. Furthermore, it encourages serious institutional efforts to turn existing English language programmes into effective avenues for raising students' English proficiency and advanced literacy skills needed for legitimate intertextual practices. Finally, it underscores the need to create ample opportunities for L2 students to engage in authentic academic writing tasks under the tutelage of faculty who can model legitimate intertextuality and socialise their tutees into the occluded aspects of appropriate and effective intertextuality.

References

Abasi, A. R., & Akbari, N. (2008). Are we encouraging patchwriting? Reconsidering the role of the pedagogical context in ESL student writers' transgressive intertextuality. *English for Specific Purposes*, *27*(3), 267–284. https://doi.org/10.1016/j.esp.2008.02.001.

Abasi, A. R., Akbari, N., & Graves, B. (2006). Discourse appropriation, construction of identities, and the complex issue of plagiarism: ESL students writing in graduate school. *Journal of Second Language Writing*, *15*(2), 102–117. https://doi.org/10.1016/j.jslw.2006.05.001.

Abasi, A. R., & Graves, B. (2008). Academic literacy and plagiarism: Conversations with international graduate students and disciplinary professors. *Journal of English for Academic Purposes*, *7*(4), 221–233. https://doi.org/10.1016/j.jeap.2008.10.010.

Adam, L., Anderson, V., & Spronken-Smith, R. (2017). 'It's not fair': Policy discourses and students' understandings of plagiarism in a New Zealand university. *Higher Education*, *74*(1), 17–32. https://doi.org/10.1007/s10734-016-0025-9.

AL Harrasi, K. T. S. (2023). Developing a needs-based plagiarism management in second-language writing in a higher education institute: Practice-oriented research. *Instructional Science*, *51*, 1079–1115. https://doi.org/10.1007/s11251-023-09628-6.

Amiri, F., & Razmjoo, S. A. (2016). On Iranian EFL undergraduate students' perceptions of plagiarism. *Journal of Academic Ethics*, *14*(2), 115–131. https://doi.org/10.1007/s10805-015-9245-3.

Angélil-Carter, S. (2000). *Stolen language?: Plagiarism in writing*. Longman.

Ashworth, P., Bannister, P., Thorne, P., & Students on the Qualitative Research Methods Course Unit. (1997). Guilty in whose eyes? University students' perceptions of cheating and plagiarism in academic work and assessment. *Studies in Higher Education*, *22*(2), 187–203. https://doi.org/10.1080/03075079712331381034.

Bakhtin, M. (1986). *Speech genres and other late essays*. University of Texas Press.

Barks, D., & Watts, P. (2001). Textual borrowing strategies for graduate-level ESL writers. In D. Belcher & A. Hirvela (Eds.), *Linking literacies: Perspectives on L2 reading-writing connections* (pp. 246–267). University of Michigan Press.

Bikowski, D., & Gui, M. (2018). The influence of culture and educational context on Chinese students' understandings of source use practices and plagiarism. *System*, *74*, 194–205. https://doi.org/10.1016/j.system.2018.03.017.

Bloch, J. (2001). Plagiarism and the ESL student: From printed to electronic texts. In D. Belcher & A. Hirvela (Eds.), *Linking literacies: Perspectives on L2 reading-writing connections* (pp. 209–228). University of Michigan Press.

Bloch, J. (2012). *Plagiarism, intellectual property and the teaching of L2 writing*. Multilingual Matters.

Borg, E. (2009). Local plagiarisms. *Assessment & Evaluation in Higher Education, 34*(4), 415–426. https://doi.org/10.1080/02602930802075115.

Bowen, N. E. J. A., & Nanni, A. (2021). Piracy, playing the system, or poor policies? Perspectives on plagiarism in Thailand. *Journal of English for Academic Purposes, 51*, 1–13. https://doi.org/10.1016/j.jeap.2021.100992.

Bretag, T. (2013). Challenges in addressing plagiarism in education. *PLoS Medicine 10*(12), 1–4. https://doi.org/10.1371/journal.pmed.1001574.

Bretag, T., & Mahmud, S. (2016). A conceptual framework for implementing exemplary academic integrity policy in Australian higher education. In T. Bretag (Ed.), *Handbook of academic integrity* (pp. 463–480). Springer. https://doi.org/10.1007/978-981-287-098-8_24.

Bretag, T., Mahmud, S., Wallace, M. et al. (2014). 'Teach us how to do it properly!' An Australian academic integrity student survey. *Studies in Higher Education, 39*(7), 1150–1169. https://doi.org/10.1080/03075079.2013.777406.

Briggs, R. (2003). Shameless! Reconceiving the problem of plagiarism. *The Australian Universities' Review, 46*(1), 19–23. https://doi/10.3316/ielapa.921535952454436.

Brimble, M., & Stevenson-Clarke, P. (2005). Perceptions of the prevalence and seriousness of academic dishonesty in Australian universities. *The Australian Educational Researcher, 32*(3), 19–44. https://doi.org/10.1007/BF03216825.

Brown, V. J., & Howell, M. E. (2001). The efficacy of policy statements on plagiarism: Do they change students' views? *Research in Higher Education, 42*(1), 103–118. https://doi.org/10.1023/A:1018720728840.

Buranen, L. (1999). But I wasn't cheating: Plagiarism and cross-cultural mythology. In L. Buranen & A. Roy (Eds.), *Perspectives on plagiarism and intellectual property in a postmodern world* (pp. 63–74). State University of New York Press.

Buranen, L., & Roy, A. (Eds.). (1999). *Perspectives on plagiarism and intellectual property in a postmodern world*. State University of New York Press.

Campbell, C. (1990). Writing with others' words: Using background reading text in academic compositions. In B. Kroll (Ed.), *Second language writing: Research insights for the classroom* (pp. 211–230). Cambridge University Press.

Chandrasegaran, A. (2000). Cultures in contact in academic writing: Students' perceptions of plagiarism. *Asian Journal of English Language Teaching, 10,* 91–113.

Chandrasoma, R., Thompson, C., & Pennycook, A. (2004). Beyond plagiarism: Transgressive and nontransgressive intertextuality. *Journal of Language, Identity & Education, 3*(3), 171–193. https://doi.org/10.1207/s15327701 jlie0303_1.

Chen, Y., & Chou, C. (2017). Are we on the same page? College students' and faculty's perception of student plagiarism in Taiwan. *Ethics & Behavior, 27* (1), 53–73. https://doi.org/10.1080/10508422.2015.1123630.

Chien, S.-C. (2017). Taiwanese college students' perceptions of plagiarism: Cultural and educational considerations. *Ethics & Behavior, 27*(2), 118–139. https://doi.org/10.1080/10508422.2015.1136219.

Choi, Y. (2012). Paraphrase practices for using sources in L2 academic writing. *English Teaching, 67,* 51–79. https://doi.org/10.15858/engtea.67.2 .201207.51.

Clarke, O., Chan, W. Y. D., Bukuru, S., Logan, J., & Wong, R. (2023). Assessing knowledge of and attitudes towards plagiarism and ability to recognize plagiaristic writing among university students in Rwanda. *Higher Education, 85*(2), 247–263. https://doi.org/10.1007/s10734-022-00830-y.

Clegg, S., & Flint, A. (2006). More heat than light: Plagiarism in its appearing. *British Journal of Sociology of Education, 27*(3), 373–387. https://doi.org/ 10.1080/01425690600750585.

Comas-Forgas, R., & Sureda-Negre, J. (2010). Academic plagiarism: Explanatory factors from students' perspective. *Journal of Academic Ethics, 8*(3), 217–232. https://doi.org/10.1007/s10805-010-9121-0.

Cotton, D. R. E., Cotton, P. A., & Shipway, J. R. (2024). Chatting and cheating: Ensuring academic integrity in the era of ChatGPT. *Innovations in Education and Teaching International, 61*(2), 228–239. https://doi.org/10.1080/ 14703297.2023.2190148.

Cumming, A., Kantor, R., Baba, K. et al. (2006). *Analysis of discourse features and verification of scoring levels for independent and integrated prototype written tasks for the new TOEFL.* Educational Testing Service.

Cumming, A., Lai, C., & Cho, H. (2016). Students' writing from sources for academic purposes: A synthesis of recent research. *Journal of English for Academic Purposes, 23,* 47–58. https://doi.org/10.1016/j.jeap.2016 .06.002.

Currie, P. (1998). Staying out of trouble: Apparent plagiarism and academic survival. *Journal of Second Language Writing, 7*(1), 1–18. https://doi.org/10.1016/S1060-3743(98)90003-0.

Deckert, G. D. (1993). Perspectives on plagiarism from ESL students in Hong Kong. *Journal of Second Language Writing, 2*(2), 131–148. https://doi.org/10.1016/1060-3743(93)90014-T.

Dehouche, N. (2021). Plagiarism in the age of massive Generative Pre-trained Transformers (GPT-3). *Ethics in Science and Environmental Politics, 21,* 17–23. https://doi.org/10.3354/esep00195.

Devlin, M. (2006). Policy, preparation, and prevention: Proactive minimization of student plagiarism. *Journal of Higher Education Policy and Management, 28*(1), 45–58. https://doi.org/10.1080/13600800500283791.

Devlin, M., & Gray, K. (2007). In their own words: A qualitative study of the reasons Australian university students plagiarize. *Higher Education Research & Development, 26*(2), 181–198. https://doi.org/10.1080/07294360701310805.

Dryden, L. M. (1999). A distant mirror or through the looking glass? Plagiarism and intellectual property in Japanese education. In L. Buranen & A. Roy (Eds.), *Perspectives on plagiarism and intellectual property in a postmodern world* (pp. 75–85). State University of New York Press.

Du, Y. (2019). Effect of an EAP unit on EFL student effective and appropriate source-use skills. *Journal of English for Academic Purposes, 40,* 53–73. https://doi.org/10.1016/j.jeap.2019.06.002.

Du, Y. (2022). Adopting critical-pragmatic pedagogy to address plagiarism in a Chinese context: An action research. *Journal of English for Academic Purposes, 57,* 1–13. https://doi.org/10.1016/j.jeap.2022.101112.

Duggan, F. (2006). Plagiarism: Prevention, practice and policy. *Assessment & Evaluation in Higher Education, 31*(2), 151–154. https://doi.org/10.1080/02602930500262452.

East, J. (2006). The problem of plagiarism in academic culture. *The International Journal for Educational Integrity, 2*(2), 16–28.

East, J. (2009). Aligning policy and practice: An approach to integrating academic integrity. *Journal of Academic Language & Learning, 3,* 38–51.

East, J. (2010). Judging plagiarism: A problem of morality and convention. *Higher Education, 59*(1), 69–83. https://doi.org/10.1007/s10734-009-9234-9.

Eaton, S. E. (2017). Comparative analysis of institutional policy definitions of plagiarism: A pan-Canadian university study. *Interchange, 48*(3), 271–281. https://doi.org/10.1007/s10780-017-9300-7.

Ehrich, J., Howard, S. J., Mu, C., & Bokosmaty, S. (2016). A comparison of Chinese and Australian university students' attitudes towards plagiarism. *Studies in Higher Education, 41*(2), 231–246. https://doi.org/10.1080/03075079.2014.927850.

Eke, D. O. (2023). ChatGPT and the rise of generative AI: Threat to academic integrity? *Journal of Responsible Technology, 13*, 1–4. https://doi.org/10.1016/j.jrt.2023.100060.

Ellery, K. (2008). Undergraduate plagiarism: A pedagogical perspective. *Assessment & Evaluation in Higher Education, 33*(5), 507–516. https://doi.org/10.1080/02602930701698918.

Flowerdew, J., & Li, Y. (2007a). Language re-use among Chinese apprentice scientists writing for publication. *Applied Linguistics, 28*(3), 440–465. https://doi.org/10.1093/applin/amm031.

Flowerdew, J., & Li, Y. (2007b). Plagiarism and second language writing in an electronic age. *Annual Review of Applied Linguistics, 27*, 161–183. https://doi.org/10.1017/S0267190508070086.

Fröhling, L., & Zubiaga, A. (2021). Feature-based detection of automated language models: Tackling GPT-2, GPT-3 and Grover. *PeerJ Computer Science, 7*, 1–23. https://doi.org/10.7717/peerj-cs.443.

Gee, J. P. (2011). *An introduction to discourse analysis: Theory and method.* Routledge.

Glendinning, I. (2014). Responses to student plagiarism in higher education across Europe. *International Journal for Educational Integrity, 10*, 4–20. https://doi.org/10.21913/IJEI.v10i1.930.

Gu, Q., & Brooks, J. (2008). Beyond the accusation of plagiarism. *System, 36*(3), 337–352. https://doi.org/10.1016/j.system.2008.01.004.

Gullifer, J., & Tyson, G. A. (2010). Exploring university students' perceptions of plagiarism: A focus group study. *Studies in Higher Education, 35*(4), 463–481. https://doi.org/10.1080/03075070903096508.

Gullifer, J. M., & Tyson, G. A. (2014). Who has read the policy on plagiarism? Unpacking students' understanding of plagiarism. *Studies in Higher Education, 39*(7), 1202–1218. https://doi.org/10.1080/03075079.2013.777412.

Hayes, N., & Introna, L. D. (2005a). Cultural values, plagiarism, and fairness: When plagiarism gets in the way of learning. *Ethics & Behavior, 15*(3), 213–231. https://doi.org/10.1207/s15327019eb1503_2.

Hayes, N., & Introna, L. D. (2005b). Systems for the production of plagiarists? The implications arising from the use of plagiarism detection systems in UK universities for Asian learners. *Journal of Academic Ethics, 3*(1), 55–73. https://doi.org/10.1007/s10805-006-9006-4.

Hirvela, A., & Du, Q. (2013). 'Why am I paraphrasing?': Undergraduate ESL writers' engagement with source-based academic writing and reading. *Journal of English for Academic Purposes, 12*(2), 87–98. https://doi.org/10.1016/j.jeap.2012.11.005.

Howard, R. M. (1993). A plagiarism pentimento. *The Journal of Teaching Writing, 11*, 233–245.

Howard, R. M. (1995). Plagiarisms, authorships, and the academic death penalty. *College English, 57*(7), 788–805. https://doi.org/10.2307/378403.

Howard, R. M. (1999). *Standing in the shadow of giants*. Ablex.

Howard, R. M. (2000). Sexuality, textuality: The cultural work of plagiarism. *College English, 62*(4), 473–491.

Howard, R., Serviss, T., & Rodrigue, T. (2010). Writing from sources, writing from sentences. *Writing and Pedagogy, 177*, 177–192. https://doi.org/10.1558/wap.v2i2.177.

Hu, G. (2015a). Dealing with unacceptable intertextuality in Chinese students' writing. *Journal of Education for Teaching, 41*(4), 439–441. https://doi.org/10.1080/02607476.2015.1080429.

Hu, G. (2015b). Research on plagiarism in second language writing: Where to from here? *Journal of Second Language Writing, 30*, 100–102. https://doi.org/10.1016/j.jslw.2015.08.004.

Hu, G., & Lei, J. (2012). Investigating Chinese university students' knowledge of and attitudes toward plagiarism from an integrated perspective. *Language Learning, 62*(3), 813–850. https://doi.org/10.1111/j.1467-9922.2011.00650.x.

Hu, G., & Lei, J. (2015). Chinese university students' perceptions of plagiarism. *Ethics & Behavior, 25*(3), 233–255. https://doi.org/10.1080/10508422.2014.923313.

Hu, G., & Lei, J. (2016). Plagiarism in English academic writing: A comparison of Chinese university teachers' and students' understandings and stances. *System, 56*, 107–118. https://doi.org/10.1016/j.system.2015.12.003.

Hu, G., & Shen, Y. (2021). Chinese university teachers' perceptions and practices regarding plagiarism: Knowledge, stance, and intertextual competence. *Ethics & Behavior, 31*(6), 433–450. https://doi.org/10.1080/10508422.2020.1776616.

Hu, G., & Sun, X. (2016). Chinese university EFL teachers' knowledge of and stance on plagiarism. *Comunicar, 24*, 29–37. https://doi.org/10.3916/C48-2016-03.

Hu, G., & Sun, X. (2017). Institutional policies on plagiarism: The case of eight Chinese universities of foreign languages/international studies. *System, 66*, 56–68. https://doi.org/10.1016/j.system.2017.03.015.

Hull, G., & Rose, M. (1989). Rethinking remediation: Toward a social-cognitive understanding of problematic reading and writing. *Written Communication, 6* (2), 139–154. https://doi.org/10.1177/0741088389006002001.

Husain, F. M., Al-Shaibani, G. K. S., & Mahfoodh, O. H. A. (2017). Perceptions of and attitudes toward plagiarism and factors contributing to plagiarism: A review of studies. *Journal of Academic Ethics, 15*(2), 167–195. https://doi.org/10.1007/s10805-017-9274-1.

Kaposi, D., & Dell, P. (2012). Discourses of plagiarism: Moralist, proceduralist, developmental and inter-textual approaches. *British Journal of Sociology of Education, 33*(6), 813–830. https://doi.org/10.1080/01425692.2012.686897.

Kayaoğlu, M. N., Erbay, Ş., Flitner, C., & Saltaş, D. (2016). Examining students' perceptions of plagiarism: A cross-cultural study at tertiary level. *Journal of Further and Higher Education, 40*(5), 682–705. https://doi.org/10.1080/0309877X.2015.1014320.

Keck, C. (2006). The use of paraphrase in summary writing: A comparison of L1 and L2 writers. *Journal of Second Language Writing, 15*(4), 261–278. https://doi.org/10.1016/j.jslw.2006.09.006.

Keck, C. (2014). Copying, paraphrasing, and academic writing development: A re-examination of L1 and L2 summarization practices. *Journal of Second Language Writing, 25*, 4–22. https://doi.org/10.1016/j.jslw.2014.05.005.

Kolich, A. M. (1983). Plagiarism: The worm of reason. *College English, 45*, 141–148.

Leask, B. (2006). Plagiarism, cultural diversity and metaphor – implications for academic staff development. *Assessment & Evaluation in Higher Education, 31*(2), 183–199. https://doi.org/10.1080/02602930500262486.

Lei, J., & Hu, G. (2014). Chinese ESOL lecturers' stance on plagiarism: Does knowledge matter? *ELT Journal, 68*(1), 41–51. https://doi.org/10.1093/elt/cct061.

Lei, J., & Hu, G. (2015). Chinese university EFL teachers' perceptions of plagiarism. *Higher Education, 70*(3), 551–565. https://doi.org/10.1007/s10734-014-9855-5.

Li, Y. (2024). *Perspectives on plagiarism in China: History, genres, and education*. Routledge.

Li, Y., & Casanave, C. P. (2012). Two first-year students' strategies for writing from sources: Patchwriting or plagiarism? *Journal of Second Language Writing, 21*(2), 165–180. https://doi.org/10.1016/j.jslw.2012.03.002.

Li, Y., & Flowerdew, J. (2018). What really is the relationship between plagiarism and culture? In D. Pecorari & P. Shaw (Eds.), *Student plagiarism in higher education* (pp. 140–156). Routledge. https://doi.org/10.4324/978131 5166148-10.

Liu, D. (2005). Plagiarism in ESOL students: Is cultural conditioning truly the major culprit? *ELT Journal, 59*(3), 234–241. https://doi.org/10.1093/elt/ cci043.

Liu, G.-Z., Lin, V., Kou, X., & Wang, H.-Y. (2016). Best practices in L2 English source use pedagogy: A thematic review and synthesis of empirical studies. *Educational Research Review, 19*, 36–57. https://doi.org/10.1016/j.edurev .2016.06.002.

Lund, B. D., Wang, T., Mannuru, N. R. et al. (2023). ChatGPT and a new academic reality: Artificial Intelligence-written research papers and the ethics of the large language models in scholarly publishing. *Journal of the Association for Information Science and Technology, 74*(5), 570–581. https://doi.org/10.1002/asi.24750.

Lundsford, A. (1999). Preface. In L. Buranen & A. Roy (Eds.), *Perspectives on plagiarism and intellectual property in a postmodern world* (pp. ix–xii). State University of New York Press.

Luzón, M. J. (2015). An analysis of the citation practices of undergraduate Spanish students. *Journal of Academic Writing, 5*, 52–64. https://doi.org/ 10.18552/joaw.v5i1.158.

Macdonald, R., & Carroll, J. (2006). Plagiarism – a complex issue requiring a holistic institutional approach. *Assessment & Evaluation in Higher Education, 31*(2), 233–245. https://doi.org/10.1080/02602930500262536.

Marshall, S., & Garry, M. (2006). NESB and ESB students' attitudes and perceptions of plagiarism. *International Journal for Educational Integrity, 2*(1), 26–37. https://doi.org/10.21913/IJEI.v2i1.25.

Matalene, C. B. (1985). Contrastive rhetoric: An American writing teacher in China. *College English, 47*, 789–808. https://doi.org/10.2307/376613.

Maxwell, A., Curtis, G., & Vardanega, L. (2008). Does culture influence understanding and perceived seriousness of plagiarism? *International Journal for Educational Integrity, 25*(4), 25–40. https://doi.org/10.21913/ IJEI.v4i2.412.

McCabe, D. L. (2001). Cheating: Why students do it and how we can help them stop. *The American Educator, 25*, 38–43.

McCabe, D. L. (2005a). Cheating among college and university students: A North American perspective. *International Journal for Educational Integrity, 1*, 1–11. https://doi.org/10.21913/IJEI.v1i1.14.

McCabe, D. L. (2005b). It takes a village: Academic dishonesty & educational opportunity. *Liberal Education, 91*, 26–31.

McCabe, D. L., & Trevino, L. K. (1997). Individual and contextual influences on academic dishonesty: A multi-campus investigation. *Research in Higher Education, 38*(3), 379–396. https://doi.org/10.1023/A:1024954224675.

McCabe, D. L., Treviño, L. K., & Butterfield, K. D. (2002). Honor codes and other contextual influences on academic integrity: A replication and extension to modified honor code settings. *Research in Higher Education, 43*(3), 357–378. https://doi.org/10.1023/A:1014893102151.

McCulloch, A., Behrend, M., & Braithwaite, F. (2022). The multiple uses of iThenticate in doctoral education: Policing malpractice or improving research writing? *Australasian Journal of Educational Technology, 38*(1), 20–32. https://doi.org/10.14742/ajet.7100.

McDonough, K., Crawford, W. J., & De Vleeschauwer, J. (2014). Summary writing in a Thai EFL university context. *Journal of Second Language Writing, 24*, 20–32. https://doi.org/10.1016/j.jslw.2014.03.001.

McKenna, S. (2022). Plagiarism and the commodification of knowledge. *Higher Education, 84*(6), 1283–1298. https://doi.org/10.1007/s10734-022-00926-5.

Merkel, W. (2021). Collage of confusion: An analysis of one university's multiple plagiarism policies. *System, 96*, 1–11. https://doi.org/10.1016/j.system.2020.102399.

Morris, E. J., & Carroll, J. (2016). Developing a sustainable holistic institutional approach: Dealing with realities 'on the ground' when implementing an academic integrity policy. In T. Bretag (Ed.), *Handbook of academic integrity* (pp. 449–462). Springer. https://doi.org/10.1007/978-981-287-098-8_23.

Moss, S. A., White, B., & Lee, J. (2018). A systematic review into the psychological causes and correlates of plagiarism. *Ethics & Behavior, 28*(4), 261–283. https://doi.org/10.1080/10508422.2017.1341837.

Nature. (2023). Tools such as ChatGPT threaten transparent science; here are our ground rules for their use. *Nature, 613*, 612. https://doi.org/10.1038/d41586-023-00191-1.

Ouellette, M. A. (2008). Weaving strands of writer identity: Self as author and the NNES "plagiarist". *Journal of Second Language Writing, 17*(4), 255–273. https://doi.org/10.1016/j.jslw.2008.05.002.

Pan, J., & Lei, J. (2024). Profiling Chinese university students' understandings of plagiarism through Q methodology. *Ethics & Behavior*, 1–16. https://doi.org/10.1080/10508422.2024.2389541.

Park, C. (2003). In other (people's) words: Plagiarism by university students—literature and lessons. *Assessment & Evaluation in Higher Education, 28*(5), 471–488. https://doi.org/10.1080/02602930301677.

Park, C. (2004). Rebels without a clause: Towards an institutional framework for dealing with plagiarism by students. *Journal of Further and Higher Education, 28*(3), 291–306. https://doi.org/10.1080/0309877042000241760.

Pecorari, D. (2001). Plagiarism and international students: How the English-speaking university responds. In D. Belcher & A. Hirvela (Eds.), *Linking literacies: Perspectives on L2 reading-writing connections* (pp. 229–245). University of Michigan Press.

Pecorari, D. (2003). Good and original: Plagiarism and patchwriting in academic second-language writing. *Journal of Second Language Writing, 12*(4), 317–345. https://doi.org/10.1016/j.jslw.2003.08.004.

Pecorari, D. (2006). Visible and occluded citation features in postgraduate second-language writing. *English for Specific Purposes, 25*(1), 4–29. https://doi.org/10.1016/j.esp.2005.04.004.

Pecorari, D. (2008). *Academic writing and plagiarism: A linguistic analysis.* Continuum.

Pecorari, D. (2013). *Teaching to avoid plagiarism: How to promote good source use.* Open University Press.

Pecorari, D. (2023). Plagiarism and English for academic purposes: A research agenda. *Language Teaching, 56*(3), 362–376. https://doi.org/10.1017/S0261444821000495.

Pecorari, D., & Petrić, B. (2014). Plagiarism in second-language writing. *Language Teaching, 47*(3), 269–302. https://doi.org/10.1017/S0261444814000056.

Pecorari, D., & Shaw, P. (2012). Types of student intertextuality and faculty attitudes. *Journal of Second Language Writing, 21*(2), 149–164. https://doi.org/10.1016/j.jslw.2012.03.006.

Pennycook, A. (1994). The complex contexts of plagiarism: A reply to Deckert. *Journal of Second Language Writing, 3*(3), 277–284. https://doi.org/10.1016/1060-3743(94)90020-5.

Pennycook, A. (1996). Borrowing others' words: Text, ownership, memory, and plagiarism. *TESOL Quarterly, 30*(2), 201–230. https://doi.org/10.2307/3588141.

Petrić, B. (2004). A pedagogical perspective on plagiarism. *NovELTy, 11*(1), 4–18.

Petrić, B. (2007). Rhetorical functions of citations in high- and low-rated master's theses. *Journal of English for Academic Purposes, 6*(3), 238–253. https://doi.org/10.1016/j.jeap.2007.09.002.

Petrić, B. (2012). Legitimate textual borrowing: Direct quotation in L2 student writing. *Journal of Second Language Writing, 21*(2), 102–117. https://doi.org/10.1016/j.jslw.2012.03.005.

Petrić, B., & Harwood, N. (2013). Task requirements, task representation, and self-reported citation functions: An exploratory study of a successful L2 student's writing. *Journal of English for Academic Purposes, 12*(2), 110–124. https://doi.org/10.1016/j.jeap.2013.01.002.

Phan, L. H. (2006). Plagiarism and overseas students: Stereotypes again? *ELT Journal, 60*(1), 76–78. https://doi.org/10.1093/elt/cci085.

Plakans, L., & Gebril, A. (2012). A close investigation into source use in integrated second language writing tasks. *Assessing Writing, 17*(1), 18–34. https://doi.org/10.1016/j.asw.2011.09.002.

Plakans, L., & Gebril, A. (2013). Using multiple texts in an integrated writing assessment: Source text use as a predictor of score. *Journal of Second Language Writing, 22*(3), 217–230. https://doi.org/10.1016/j.jslw.2013.02.003.

Power, L. G. (2009). University students' perceptions of plagiarism. *The Journal of Higher Education, 80*(6), 643–662. www.jstor.org/stable/27750755.

Price, M. (2002). Beyond 'gotcha!': Situating plagiarism in policy and pedagogy. *College Composition and Communication, 54*(1), 88–115. https://doi.org/10.2307/1512103.

Quah, C. H., Stewart, N., & Lee, J. W. C. (2012). Attitudes of business students' toward plagiarism. *Journal of Academic Ethics, 10*(3), 185–199. https://doi.org/10.1007/s10805-012-9157-4.

Rinnert, C., & Kobayashi, H. (2005). Borrowing words and ideas: Insights from Japanese L1 writers. *Journal of Asian Pacific Communication, 15*, 15–29.

Robillard, A. E., & Howard, R. M. (2008). Introduction: Plagiarism. In R. M. Howard & A. E. Robillard (Eds.), *Pluralizing plagiarism: Identities, contexts, pedagogies* (pp. 1–7). Boynton/Cook.

Roig, M. (2001). Plagiarism and paraphrasing criteria of college and university professors. *Ethics & Behavior, 11*(3), 307–323. https://doi.org/10.1207/S15327019EB1103_8.

Roy, A. (1999). Whose words these are I think I know: Plagiarism, the postmodern, and faculty attitudes. In L. Buranen & A. Roy (Eds.), *Perspectives on plagiarism and intellectual property in a postmodern world* (pp. 55–61). State University of New York Press.

Sapp, D. A. (2002). Towards an international and intercultural understanding of plagiarism and academic dishonesty in composition: Reflections from the People's Republic of China. *Issues in Writing, 13*, 58–79.

Scollon, R. (1995). Plagiarism and ideology: Identity in intercultural discourse. *Language in Society, 24*(1), 1–28. https://doi.org/10.1017/S0047404500018388.

Selwyn, N. (2008). 'Not necessarily a bad thing . . . ': A study of online plagiarism amongst undergraduate students. *Assessment & Evaluation in Higher Education, 33*(5), 465–479. https://doi.org/10.1080/02602930701563104.

Shen, Y., & Hu, G. (2021). Chinese graduate students' perceptions of plagiarism: A mixed-methods study. *Accountability in Research, 28*(4), 197–225. https://doi.org/10.1080/08989621.2020.1819253.

Sherman, J. (1992). Your own thoughts in your own words. *ELT Journal, 46*(2), 190–198. https://doi.org/10.1093/elt/46.2.190.

Shi, L. (2004). Textual borrowing in second-language writing. *Written Communication, 21*(2), 171–200. https://doi.org/10.1177/0741088303262846.

Shi, L. (2006). Cultural backgrounds and textual appropriation. *Language Awareness, 15*(4), 264–282. https://doi.org/10.2167/la406.0.

Shi, L. (2010). Textual appropriation and citing behaviors of university undergraduates. *Applied Linguistics, 31*(1), 1–24. https://doi.org/10.1093/applin/amn045.

Shi, L. (2012). Rewriting and paraphrasing source texts in second language writing. *Journal of Second Language Writing, 21*(2), 134–148. https://doi.org/10.1016/j.jslw.2012.03.003.

Song-Turner, H. (2008). Plagiarism: Academic dishonesty or 'blind spot' of multicultural education? *Australian Universities' Review, 50*, 39–50.

Sowden, C. (2005). Plagiarism and the culture of multilingual students in higher education abroad. *ELT Journal, 59*(3), 226–233. https://doi.org/10.1093/elt/cci042.

Stapleton, P. (2012). Gauging the effectiveness of anti-plagiarism software: An empirical study of second language graduate writers. *Journal of English for Academic Purposes, 11*(2), 125–133. https://doi.org/10.1016/j.jeap.2011.10.003.

Starfield, S. (2002). 'I'm a second-language English speaker': Negotiating writer identity and authority in sociology one. *Journal of Language, Identity & Education, 1*(2), 121–140. https://doi.org/10.1207/S15327701JLIE0102_02.

Stokel-Walker, C. (2023). ChatGPT listed as author on research papers: Many scientists disapprove. *Nature, 613*, 620–621. https://doi.org/10.1038/d41586-023-00107-z.

Sun, Y.-C. (2009). Using a two-tier test in examining Taiwan graduate students' perspectives on paraphrasing strategies. *Asia Pacific Education Review, 10*(3), 399–408. https://doi.org/10.1007/s12564-009-9035-y.

Sun, Y.-C. (2012). Does text readability matter? A study of paraphrasing and plagiarism in English as a foreign language writing context. *Asia-Pacific Education Researcher, 21*, 296–306.

Sun, X., & Hu, G. (2020). What do academics know and do about plagiarism? An interview study with Chinese university teachers of English. *Ethics & Behavior*, *30*(6), 459–479. https://doi.org/10.1080/10508422.2019.1633922.

Sun, X., & Hu, G. (2024). Institutional policies on plagiarism management: A comparison of universities in mainland China and Hong Kong. *Accountability in Research*, *31*(4), 281–304. https://doi.org/10.1080/08989621.2022.2120390.

Sutherland-Smith, W. (2005). Pandora's box: Academic perceptions of student plagiarism in writing. *Journal of English for Academic Purposes*, *4*(1), 83–95. https://doi.org/10.1016/j.jeap.2004.07.007.

Sutherland-Smith, W. (2008). *Plagiarism, the internet and student learning: Improving academic integrity*. Routledge. https://doi.org/10.4324/9780203928370.

Sutherland-Smith, W. (2010). Retribution, deterrence and reform: The dilemmas of plagiarism management in universities. *Journal of Higher Education Policy and Management*, *32*(1), 5–16. https://doi.org/10.1080/13600800903440519.

Sutherland-Smith, W. (2011). Crime and punishment: An analysis of university plagiarism policies. *Semiotica*, *187*(1/4), 127–139. https://doi.org/10.1515/semi.2011.067.

Sutherland-Smith, W. (2014). Legality, quality assurance and learning: Competing discourses of plagiarism management in higher education. *Journal of Higher Education Policy and Management*, *36*(1), 29–42. https://doi.org/10.1080/1360080X.2013.844666.

Sutherland-Smith, W., & Carr, R. (2005). Turnitin.com: Teachers' perspectives of anti-plagiarism software in raising issues of educational integrity. *Journal of University Teaching & Learning Practice*, *2*(3), 106–114. https://doi.org/10.53761/1.2.3.10.

Sutton, A., & Taylor, D. (2011). Confusion about collusion: Working together and academic integrity. *Assessment & Evaluation in Higher Education*, *36*(7), 831–841. https://doi.org/10.1080/02602938.2010.488797.

Thompson, C., Morton, J., & Storch, N. (2013). Where from, who, why and how? A study of the use of sources by first year L2 university students. *Journal of English for Academic Purposes*, *12*(2), 99–109. https://doi.org/10.1016/j.jeap.2012.11.004.

Tomaš, Z. (2010). Addressing pedagogy on textual borrowing: Focus on instructional resources. *Writing & Pedagogy*, *2*(2), 223–250. https://doi.org/10.1558/wap.v2i2.223.

Tremayne, K., & Curtis, G. J. (2021). Attitudes and understanding are only part of the story: Self-control, age and self-imposed pressure predict plagiarism over and above perceptions of seriousness and understanding. *Assessment &*

Evaluation in Higher Education, 46(2), 208–219. https://doi.org/10.1080/02602938.2020.1764907.

Valentine, K. (2006). Plagiarism as literacy practice: Recognizing and rethinking ethical binaries. *College Composition and Communication, 58*(1), 89–109.

Walker, J. (2010). Measuring plagiarism: Researching what students do, not what they say they do. *Studies in Higher Education, 35*(1), 41–59. https://doi.org/10.1080/03075070902912994.

Walker, C., & White, M. (2014). Police, design, plan and manage: Developing a framework for integrating staff roles and institutional policies into a plagiarism prevention strategy. *Journal of Higher Education Policy and Management, 36* (6), 674–687. https://doi.org/10.1080/1360080X.2014.957895.

Weber-Wulff, D., Anohina-Naumeca, A., Bjelobaba, S. et al. (2023). Testing of detection tools for AI-generated text. *International Journal for Educational Integrity, 19*(1), 1–39. https://doi.org/10.1007/s40979-023-00146-z.

Wette, R. (2010). Evaluating student learning in a university-level EAP unit on writing using sources. *Journal of Second Language Writing, 19*(3), 158–177. https://doi.org/10.1016/j.jslw.2010.06.002.

Wette, R. (2021). *Writing using sources for academic purposes: Theory, research, and practice*. Routledge.

Wheeler, G. (2009). Plagiarism in the Japanese universities: Truly a cultural matter? *Journal of Second Language Writing, 18*(1), 17–29. https://doi.org/10.1016/j.jslw.2008.09.004.

Whitley, B. E. (1998). Factors associated with cheating among college students: A review. *Research in Higher Education, 39*(3), 235–274. https://doi.org/10.1023/A:1018724900565.

Yang, R., Hu, G., & Lei, J. (2023). Understanding Chinese English-major students' intertextual competence and contributing factors. *Assessment & Evaluation in Higher Education, 48*(5), 657–671. https://doi.org/10.1080/02602938.2022.2102137.

Yeo, S. (2007). First-year university science and engineering students' understanding of plagiarism. *Higher Education Research & Development, 26*(2), 199–216. https://doi.org/10.1080/07294360701310813.

Zafarghandi, A. M., Khoshroo, F., & Barkat, B. (2012). An investigation of Iranian EFL Masters students' perceptions of plagiarism. *The International Journal for Educational Integrity, 8*, 69–85.

Zhang, Y., Chu, S. K. W., Qiu, X., Zainuddin, Z., & Li, X. (2024). Facilitating undergraduates' plagiarism-free academic writing practices in a blended learning scenario. *Innovations in Education and Teaching International, 61* (1), 154–167. https://doi.org/10.1080/14703297.2022.2102529.

Cambridge Elements ☰

Applied Linguistics

Li Wei
University College London

Li Wei is Chair of Applied Linguistics at the UCL Institute of Education, University College London (UCL), and Fellow of Academy of Social Sciences, UK. His research covers different aspects of bilingualism and multilingualism. He was the founding editor of the following journals: *International Journal of Bilingualism* (Sage), *Applied Linguistics Review* (De Gruyter), *Language, Culture and Society* (Benjamins), *Chinese Language and Discourse* (Benjamins) and *Global Chinese* (De Gruyter), and is currently Editor of the *International Journal of Bilingual Education and Bilingualism* (Taylor and Francis). His books include the *Blackwell Guide to Research Methods in Bilingualism and Multilingualism* (with Melissa Moyer) and *Translanguaging: Language, Bilingualism and Education* (with Ofelia Garcia) which won the British Association of Applied Linguistics Book Prize.

Zhu Hua
University College London

Zhu Hua is Professor of Language Learning and Intercultural Communication at the UCL Institute of Education, University College London (UCL) and is a Fellow of Academy of Social Sciences, UK. Her research is centred around multilingual and intercultural communication. She has also studied child language development and language learning. She is book series co-editor for *Routledge Studies in Language and Intercultural Communication* and *Cambridge Key Topics in Applied Linguistics*, and Forum and Book Reviews Editor of *Applied Linguistics* (Oxford University Press).

About the Series

Mirroring the Cambridge Key Topics in Applied Linguistics, this Elements series focuses on the key topics, concepts and methods in Applied Linguistics today. It revisits core conceptual and methodological issues in different subareas of Applied Linguistics. It also explores new emerging themes and topics. All topics are examined in connection with real-world issues and the broader political, economic and ideological contexts.

Cambridge Elements ≡

Applied Linguistics

Elements in the Series

A full series listing is available at: www.cambridge.org/EIAL

Printed in the United States
by Baker & Taylor Publisher Services

Printed in the United States
by Baker & Taylor Publisher Services